The Legend of the Linden:
A HISTORY OF SLOVAKIA

"Every nation will rise under God's sun and the Linden blossoms long after the Oak has wilted"

Ľudovít Štúr

Slavdom and the World of the Future

The Legend of the Linden: A History of Slovakia @2020
By Zuzana Palovic and Gabriela Bereghazyova
All Rights Reserved

Second Edition
The Legend of the Linden: A History of Slovakia @2020
Published by Global Slovakia, Bratislava, Slovakia, All Rights
Reserved
Co-Published by Hybrid Global Publishing, 301 E 57th Street,
4th FL, New York City, New York, 10022 USA
Paperback ISBN: 978-1-951943-26-4
Ebook ISBN: 978-1-951943-27-1

First Edition
The Legend of the Linden: A History of Slovakia
Published by Global Slovakia,
Bratislava, Slovakia
ISBN 978-1-78808-067-5

Concept: Zuzana Palovic and Gabriela Bereghazyova
Text: Zuzana Palovic and Gabriela Bereghazyova
Book Graphic Design: Jacqueline Auty
Illustrations: Zuzana Smatlakova
Photography: Iva Simkova; Zuzana Burdanova;
Jacqueline Auty; Michalis Pastrikos;
Ladislav Bielik; Online Archives

Manufactured in the United States of America, or in the United Kingdom when distributed elsewhere.

Library of Congress cataloging-in-publication data available upon request.

www.globalslovakia.com

CONTENTS

CONCLUSION

EPILOGUE

AUTHORS' AFTERWORD

The Legend of the Linden:
A HISTORY OF SLOVAKIA

FOREWORD BY JURAJ JAKUBISKO:
MY LEGEND ABOUT THE MAGICAL
COUNTRY OF THE LINDEN

I know about my birth from the tales of my mother. On the night before May Day, crows brought me from across the mountain to Kojšov. My mother was the only woman still awake and so they left me in her embrace and flew away. The tiny village hidden amongst the hills and forests of Slovakia became my birth cradle.

Even though Kojšov was more hospitable to pine trees, a few Linden trees grew there as well. Just like in every other village. The mightiest one stood in front of a church. One day, through the forest, came a wandering photographer. Our mayor stood a chair underneath the Linden and all the village's children had their first-ever photograph taken. I was two years old and incredibly proud of it. Back then, I did not know that my village and I were part of the grand and mysterious realm of the Slavs. Nor did I know that we are their children, raised on our ancestor's songs, fairy tales, rituals and love.

The emblem of the Linden has been with me since early childhood, through both good and bad. My very first packet of cigarettes were called 'Lindens'. The money coin which would occasionally roll into my hands had a Linden shoot on it. In the Bratislava art school that I attended, the Linden branch was the most popular study. In the film *Sitting on a Branch, Enjoying Myself*, my heroes would hide in the crown of a Linden to shield themselves from an uncertain world. When I met Federico Fellini, who called me his friend and brother, I discovered that as a child, he too sought refuge in a tree from the world of adults.

The only difference was the type of tree that each one of us, just as each culture, was drawn to. For example, the Germans chose the great oak with its powerful roots and robust branches to express their strength.

The Slavic, and so the Slovak, Linden stretches as far and wide as the Slav family and it is as abundant as their soul. Perhaps that is why its leaves resemble hearts. Overflowing with white blossom in spring, ready for harvest by late summer, only for autumn to come and swirl them like tiny propellers towards the soil to become a remedy against the cold breath of winter.

I often say that Slovakia is a land of miracles. However, my life in it has not always been easy. Just like my country, I too experienced a lot of pain. Sometimes it seemed that not even the grand Linden of my ancestors was a cure strong enough to heal my broken heart.

I could not make films for ten years during communism. In spite of that I refused to leave my homeland and persevered until a time came when politics stopped being an obstacle to art. When I could once again shoot movies, their stories were always marked by the magic of the Slavs. With them I travelled the world, a realm I once thought was but a story for children. My greatest desire was to spread word of the beauty of my country and the diligence of her people. But above all, I wanted the world to know of the great Slavic soul and the wisdom of our eternal traditions, breathing through every leaf of the beloved Linden.

My journey through the realm of film is coming to an end. The time has come to honour the deepest and most enigmatic roots of my motherland. Like the authors of this exceptional book, my being also longs to celebrate the Slovak essence in its purest and most sacred form. I too desire to contribute to Slovak self-discovery through that which I do best.

The film *Slavic Epopee* is the story of Great Moravia and its king Svätopluk. The tale of a great man who built an empire, influenced the history of Europe, but failed to raise a successor, offers a timeless message to the world. The Linden is at the heart of the saga as the silent witness to Svätopluk's triumphs and sorrows. After all, it was around this sacred tree that the ancestors of the Slovaks built wooden churches, the spiritual centres of the empire.

Every endeavour that strives to leave behind knowledge of where we came from, where we are going, how far our roots reach and what we can be proud of, warms my heart. *The Legend of the Linden: A History of Slovakia* is an important and beautiful part of this collective effort. It serves as a reminder to Slovaks. Its gentle voice assures us that we belong and that we always have a place to return to after our worldly wanders. It vows that the ancient Linden will never deny us her soothing embrace.

Juraj Jakubisko

Iconic Slovak Film Director & National Treasure

LET THERE BE LIGHT...

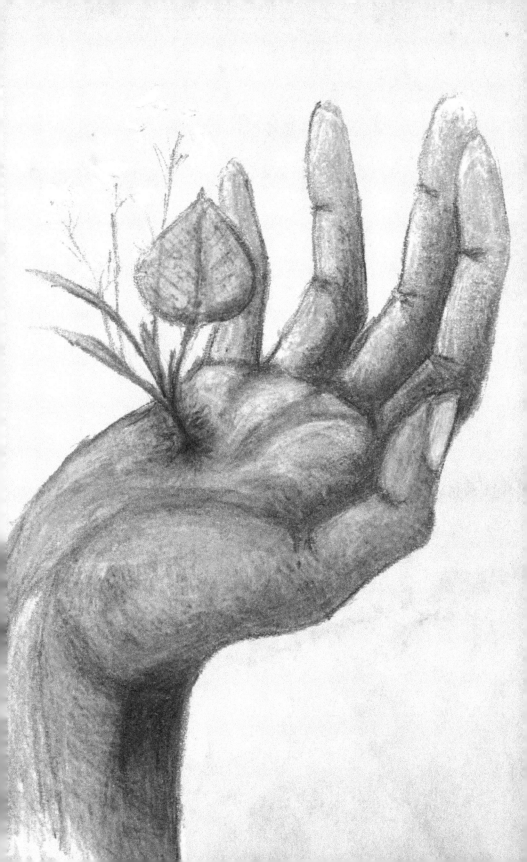

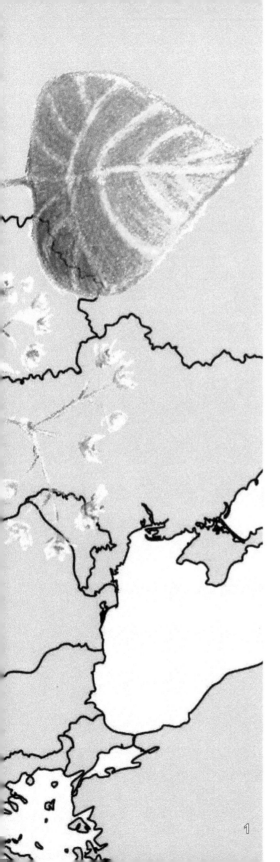

PRELUDE:

SLOVAKIA IS SITUATED IN THE VERY HEART OF EUROPE

You are reading a little known, yet important story. It is a tale of a once invisible nation that lay unnoticed in the heart of Europe for much of recorded human history. Hidden away, its spellbinding secret kept growing and maturing. The land that we know as Slovakia today is the bearer of this untamed and undiscovered glory.

SLOVAKIA

may be a young country, but the Slovaks are an old people. Theirs is a dramatic journey that began long before the dawn of Christianity. Slovaks are the descendants of the mystical Slavs, the free-spirited people who long ago merged with the soil and essence of the land. Their legacy is forever immortalized in the very name 'Slovakia' and lives on in the blood of the people that call this country home.

It was not until the turn of the third millennium, that Slovakia was finally reclaimed by the surviving progeny of the ancient Slavs as a sovereign country and nation. After so many centuries of struggle and escapes from annihilation at the hands of many foreign interests, sovereignty came on a cold and unforgettable January 1st 1993. Standing in unity, the Slovaks cried with joy as their national flag kissed the sky in freedom for the very first time.

How did such a small nation survive through all these perils? How is it possible that the Slovaks prevailed to see the dawn of the 21st century as a strong, independent and thriving country?

INTRODUCTION:
THE SACRED LINDEN CODE

The land that we know as Slovakia today is protected by an all-powerful symbol, the Linden tree and its heart-shaped leaf. For centuries, the sacred icon has represented the heartfelt essence of the Slovak people. It is a code that captures the narrative of a nation. The heart-shaped emblem masterfully unites the humanity, geography and heritage of the region.

IF
YOU
SEEK

to understand the enigmatic world
of the Slovaks, you must dare to take
a leap of faith. Using reason alone is
not enough to decode the meaning of
the Linden. To enter a world guided
by the emotional language of the tree
symbol, you need to venture into the
astounding world of your own heart
and soul.

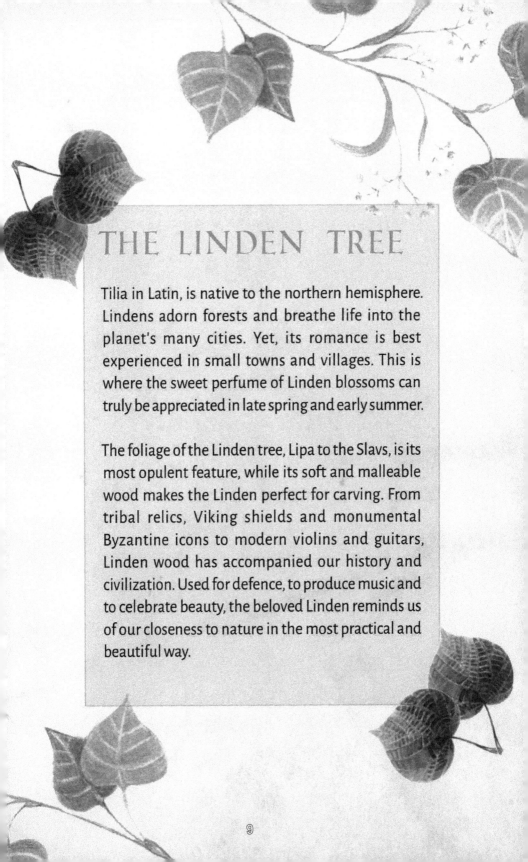

THE LINDEN TREE

Tilia in Latin, is native to the northern hemisphere. Lindens adorn forests and breathe life into the planet's many cities. Yet, its romance is best experienced in small towns and villages. This is where the sweet perfume of Linden blossoms can truly be appreciated in late spring and early summer.

The foliage of the Linden tree, Lipa to the Slavs, is its most opulent feature, while its soft and malleable wood makes the Linden perfect for carving. From tribal relics, Viking shields and monumental Byzantine icons to modern violins and guitars, Linden wood has accompanied our history and civilization. Used for defence, to produce music and to celebrate beauty, the beloved Linden reminds us of our closeness to nature in the most practical and beautiful way.

The Linden produces pale sweet-smelling clusters of flowers that are much beloved by bees. Linden **pollen** is a key ingredient in Slovakia's most popular type of honey. Even more importantly, it is critical to the agriculture of not only Slovakia, but of the entire Northern hemisphere.

Farmers knew this and for thousands of years they planted Linden trees to attract **bees.** Honey is a by-product of the pollination process, without which Slovak, European and global agriculture would be doomed. Bees and their tree, the Linden growing across the world, are crucial to our survival as a species.

Not only does the Linden produce **sweet honey**, its blossoms have medicinal properties too. They ease colds and flus and are a strong, yet gentle, natural pain reliever. Doctors often recommend tea made from dried **Linden flowers** to reduce stress and anxiety. The great Linden is also well-known to the cosmetic industry that uses extracts from its flowers and wood in lotions, creams and massage oils.

The dew of the last word of the last page of this book will anoint you as a keeper of the **Linden** tale. For once the gentle leaf has landed in your hand, its **alchemy** unlocks the secret door to the empire of the Slavic soul. May you embrace its **secret,** may you cherish its mystery. For the time has come to join the legacy of the Slavs in the very **heart** of Europe.

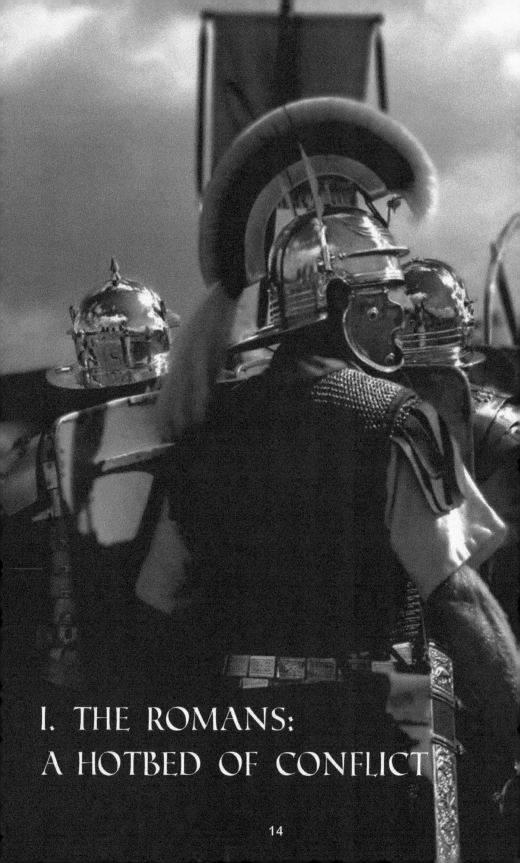

I. THE ROMANS:
A HOTBED OF CONFLICT

Located in the very **beating heart** of the continent, Slovakia has always been caught in the turmoil of perennial change. Since the very beginning, it has been a bone of contention among Europe's mightiest empires. The **Ambitious Romans** were one of the first occupiers. Their quest for even more colonies brought them to the territory in the 1st century AD. They came with the sole goal of bringing the strategic landmass under the **Emperor's control**. This did not come without confrontations with the militant Germanic tribes who did not want to miss out on the **precious land** and influence in the region.

A string of battles broke out on the fringes of the Roman world. It was the Romans who emerged victorious. Better armed and stronger in strategy and numbers, they soon absorbed the heart of Europe as part of the vast Roman **empire**.

Wherever they went, the Romans brought with them the phenomenon of the written language. This was a world where literacy was a privilege of the very few and exercising its power was the most potent weapon of all. The Romans used the written word to strengthen their glory and secure their place in the records of history.

It was the Romans who gave Slovakia its first ever written artefact. Prosaic, yet symbolic, the Roman inscription on the rock in the province of Laugaricio (Trenčín today) commemorates their military achievement. The inscription reads: "To the victory of emperors, dedicated by 855 soldiers of II. Legion of an army stationed in Laugaricio. Made to order of Marcus Valerius Maximianus, a legate of the Second Auxiliary legion."

ORIAE
STORV
CVLAV
SEDIIMIL

Following the Roman triumph, Slovakia formed the Empire's northern-most frontier on the continent. It constituted the buffer zone between the civilized Roman empire and the rest of what Romans believed to be a barbarian and untamed Europe. These events marked the beginning of Slovakia's long history of see-sawing at the crossroads of civilizations and conflicting worlds.

The Linden mysteriously infused the hearts and minds of anyone who crossed the land, regardless of their political, cultural or religious allegiance. Even through warfare, the heart-shaped Linden leaf brought solace to friends and foes across the region as both the Germanic tribes and the Roman conquerors revered the Linden as their sacred tree.

Imprints of their love affair and fascination with the Linden can be observed in the literature and mythology of the era. In both cultures, the tree embodied the female face of God. With their passing, the symbol continued to persevere and survive across many more transformations as the murky centuries of ancient Europe broke into the medieval era.

II. THE SLAVS: ANCESTORS OF THE SLOVAKS

Many peoples fleetingly passed through the country during the centuries until, one day, the wheel of fortune took hold of a new destiny. A tribe had come to stay. It was the mystical Slavs, the ancient and pagan people, who once danced, loved and united so freely around the trees, rivers and mountains of the land that is now Slovakia.

They stayed and miraculously outlived the many natural disasters and human follies that plagued the heart of Europe for centuries. These ancient Slavs live on in the blood of the modern Slovaks of today. Together they represent the region's most continuous genetic line and culture.

WHO ARE THE SLAVS?

Where did they come from and when? The truth is that we know very little about the people from the very heart of the most well-known continent in the world. Although we have dedicated much effort to studying the ancient Greeks, the spectacular Romans and even the faraway Egyptians, the Slavic heritage remains as elusive today as ever.

The commonly accepted story is that the Slavs came from beyond the Caucasus and entered Europe in the 6th century AD. Others argue that this theory is false, and that the Slavs staked their claim on the Eastern half of the old continent long before that. As the experts quarrel, The Slavs remain Europe's least documented ethnic group.

THE MYSTERY OF THE SLAVS

is partly down to the fact that Slavonic languages remained spoken, rather than written, for a very long time. This meant that their history and cultural traditions were conveyed orally. There are no written records that would help us understand the tribe. To make matters even more complicated, the Slavs left behind very few material traces for archeologists to puzzle over.

But there is also another reason why we, a species obsessed with knowing and exposing everything, know so little about the Slavs, even as we enter the 21st century. It was only very recently that the artificial barrier that separated the Slavs from the rest of the world was torn down. For much of recent history, the Iron Curtain not only brutally disrupted the connection between East and West, it also gave rise to an amnesia that people are just now slowly waking from.

THE TERRITORY OF THE SLAVS

stretches far and wide even today. It spans two continents, starting from the heart of Europe and reaching across the Caucasus, through the vastness of Russia's steppe and all the way to the Sea of Japan.

Further north, the Slavs also share a maritime border with the United States. This simple fact defies our conservative understanding of the geopolitical division of the world, and the stark separation of East and West. The shared sea border proves that we have far more in common than that which divides us.

In the world, there are 13 countries that are considered to be officially Slavic nation states. Slavic countries make up over 50% of Europe's territory which makes them the largest ethno-linguistic group on the continent. Slavic languages are spoken by more than 300 million people. Although lesser known than their Latin and Germanic counterparts, Slavic languages make up the most widely spoken language group in Europe. Due to the number of their speakers, they can be seen as the continent's unofficial lingua franca.

W hat we do know about the Slavs is that nature was paramount to their way of life. They were tribal and egalitarian. Nature shaped and informed their identity. It was the force that guided and inspired their collective journey. Nature also played a central role in their myths and stories.

The ancient Slavs chose the heart-shaped Linden leaf as their most sacred symbol and revered it as a talisman and protector of the people. The tree was also a totem and microcosm of the universe. According to the belief structure of the pagan Slavs, the Linden represented what in western tradition is known as the concept of 'as above, so below'.

Their sacred tree was believed to be indestructible. The Lipa could not be struck by lightning which is why the Slavs sought its protection in storms.

THE HISTORY of the heart

of Europe goes back thousands of years. As a result, this landscape was shared by many peoples and cultures. Long before the Slavs, the region was settled by the Celts in the 5th century BC. Remarkably the Celts, just like the later Slavs, shared an affinity with the sacred Linden tree and its heart-shaped leaf.

A testimony to this alliance is an ancient coin excavated in the capital of Slovakia, Bratislava. It depicts Biatec, the king of the Celts, riding a stallion while victoriously holding a branch of the Linden tree. This little artefact speaks volumes about the influence of the tree on the hearts and minds of the people in the region.

Today, this Celtic lineage merges with Slavic tradition in the modern story of Slovakia. The very same symbolism lives on in the emblem of the Slovak National Bank. An enlarged bronze sculpture of the coin, weighing over 3 tons, adorns the Bank's headquarters in Bratislava. It is an everyday reminder of just how much the Linden tree has enriched the lives of past and present day Slovakia and her people.

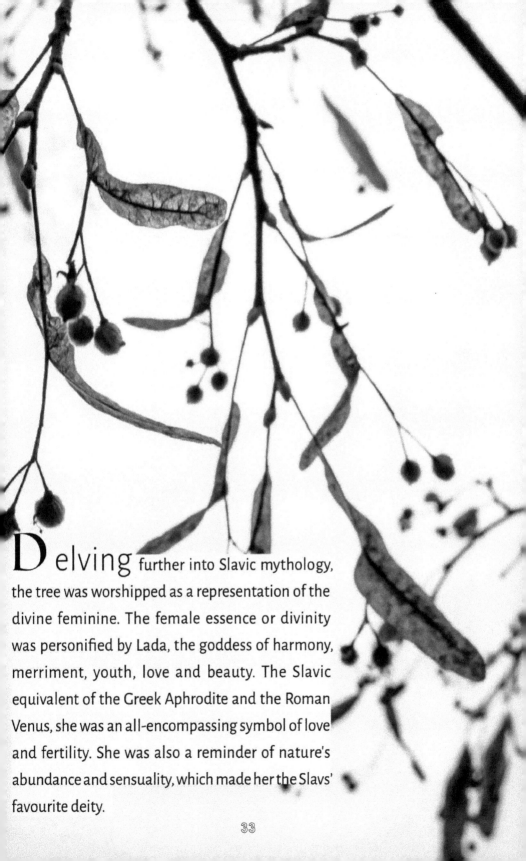

D elving further into Slavic mythology, the tree was worshipped as a representation of the divine feminine. The female essence or divinity was personified by Lada, the goddess of harmony, merriment, youth, love and beauty. The Slavic equivalent of the Greek Aphrodite and the Roman Venus, she was an all-encompassing symbol of love and fertility. She was also a reminder of nature's abundance and sensuality, which made her the Slavs' favourite deity.

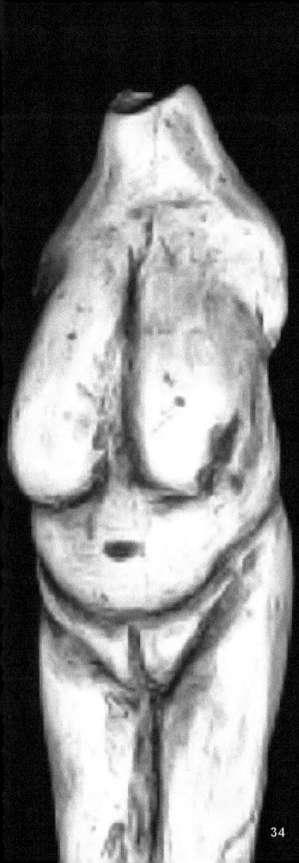

The tradition o

Worshipping the

female aspect of god, or divine

feminine, dates back ever

further to the hunters and

gatherers who once roamed

this planet. A beautiful artefac

records the presence of these

early humans, who were

perhaps the first to be drawn to

the rivers, hot springs, caves and

forests of the abundant Slovak

countryside. They left a tiny, bu

touching reminder of their life

here. Some 20,000 years old

the stunning female figurine

carved from a mammoth bone

is one of Europe's oldest relics.

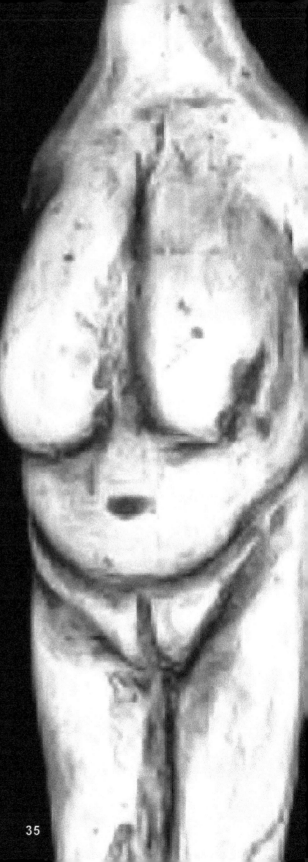

The Venus of Moravia is a primordial representation of the ancient cult of the goddess that continued to be worshipped long after that civilization vanished. It was first expressed in the form of this naked and voluptuous woman, and later overtaken by the Linden tree, personified by the goddess Lada. Others find this very same lineage embodied in the Virgin Mary, Slovakia's most popular female saint. Regardless of your preference, all three represent the region's age-old tradition of female deity worship.

III. GREAT MORAVIA: THE FORGOTTEN SLAVIC KINGDOM

As omnipresent as the Linden symbolism was in this corner of the world, it was not until the emergence of Great Moravia around 833, Europe's half-forgotten Slavic kingdom, that the Linden truly became the institutional icon of the region.

It was under the sweet blossoms of the Linden tree that the first state of the Slavs was conceived. Here, decision-makers congregated and important matters of state were decided. In the cool shadow of the Lipa, Great Moravians handed wisdom and memories to one another like gifts.

THE Great Moravian Kingdom was a remarkable achievement. It formed the institutional basis for a greatly strengthened position of the Slavs in the heart of Europe. These solid foundations allowed their influence and power to grow even more quickly. At the peak of its glory, the Great Moravian territory reached as far as modern-day Poland in the North and Romania in the South. Built up through alliances, but also conquests, the force and rise of Great Moravia was made possible through none other than the Linden tree. Its power was sealed in the shields of the Great Moravian knights, made of Linden wood.

As word of their success spread across the continent, Great Moravia also quickly became a threat to existing interests. The Francs in the West became more and more suspicious as their neighbour gained in strength and power. So were the Byzantines, the masters of the East. At the time, political divisions in Europe were underlined by religious allegiances. The Frankish Empire was associated with Catholic Rome. While their Byzantine rivals were the beating heart of the Orthodox Church.

Soon, both Eastern and Western factions set their sights on the great land of the Lipa. They shared the same ambition – to **dominate Europe.** The Franks made the first bold step by placing a puppet ruler on the Great Moravian throne. It had been emptied as a result of a **war** from which they had emerged as victors. This move proved to be a fatal mistake.

Rastislav of Moravia may have acquired the crown as a mere servant of the Frankish king, but he was also a man with a mind and **game plan** of his own. What the Franks did not know was that Rastislav, although appointed by them, held a far greater affection for and loyalty to his fellow Slavic people, than to the distant ruler. It was in their honour and for their future that he crafted a **grand vision.**

Up until **R**astislav's **coronation**, the Great Moravians were still pagans who lived life roaming freely in the harmonious cycle of nature. Close to a millennium after the birth of Christianity, this way of life was archaic and increasingly eroded.

These were the times when political power became firmly connected with the influence of the church. Rastislav was quick to recognise that governing a pagan nation was a mark of backwardness that inhibited the region's future and prosperity. He understood that the modernisation of Great Moravia was inescapable. The empire had to be Christianised to compete with the power houses of Europe and establish itself as a great Slavic entity.

44

As divine power went hand in hand with earthly influence, the opening of the kingdom to the new **Christian religion** was wrought with political interests. Nowhere was the situation as explosive as in the geopolitically critical land in the centre of Europe.

Rastislav's kingdom was wedged between the Frankish empire in the West and the power-hungry Byzantines in the East. A conflict ensued and in the end, it was Byzantium rather than the Franks and their ally Rome that would make the first and very **influential inroads** into the unknown Slavic world.

The Byzantines succeeded because their conquest did not take the form of a military invasion. Instead, the **Byzantines** sought to earn the hearts and minds of the Great Moravian people through the vehicle of religion.

Invited to Great Moravia by King Rastislav himself, two leading thinkers were selected to embark on this mission. The controversial and highly sensitive move was intended to ward off the Franks lurking around the borders of his kingdom.

Upon their arrival in 863, St. Constantine and St. Methodius did something rather astonishing. By studying and understanding the mindset and beliefs of the local people, the two monks managed to introduce Christianity, a whole new belief system, to the then illiterate people.

MODERN SLOVAKIA

is a living reminder of the ancient religious competition between East and West. Today, the small country in the heart of Europe constitutes a dividing line between the Latin West and the Greek East, that is between the Catholic and Orthodox Churches. An existence at the crossroads of beliefs is immortalised in Slovak stone.

The dividing line of Eastern and Western Christendom is reflected in the sacral architecture of the country. The wooden churches and onion shaped towers in the East of Slovakia remind us of Byzantium. The monumental architecture of the Catholic Church scattered throughout the country takes us back to the days of the Holy Roman Empire of the Franks.

Both sides of the divide brought the Linden into the interiors of their sacred spaces. While the statues embellishing Roman Catholic Churches are often carved from linden wood, the icons of the Eastern Orthodoxy are painted on Linden panels. Wherever you look, both inside and outside the sacred monuments, the Linden tree is never far.

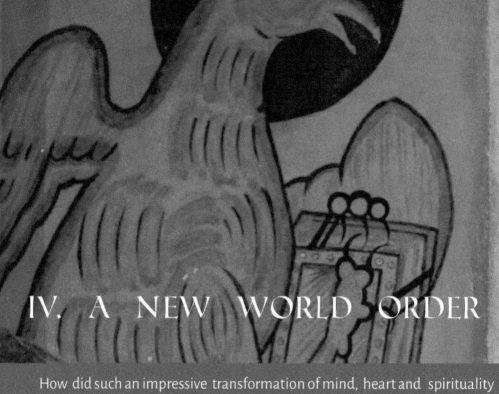

IV. A NEW WORLD ORDER

How did such an impressive transformation of mind, heart and spirituality take place so quickly? It was all made possible by bringing to the Slavs of Great Moravia something that they had been missing. The written language.

Constantine and his brother Methodius knew they needed to present Christianity in the language of the people. They knew that in order to persuade the Slavs to abandon their pagan beliefs without resistance or violence, they had to make Christianity accessible. First and foremost, they had to translate the Bible. To do this, they had to create written Slavonic. And so, the brothers gave the spoken Slavonic its first ever alphabet. It was a stroke of genius.

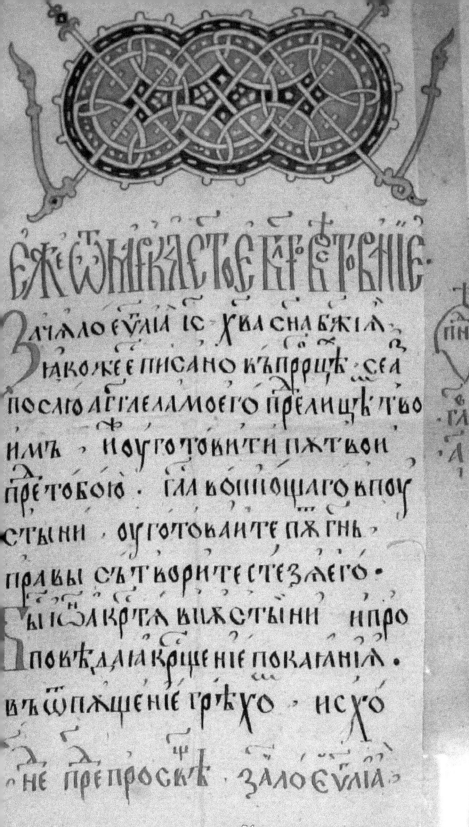

ЕЖЕ Ѡ НЕКЛАСТ Е КРЕ СТВНІЕ ·

ЗАЧАЛО ЕѴЛІА ІС ХВА СНА БЖІА ·
ЯКОЖЕ Е ПИСАНО КЪ ПРЦЪ · СЕ А
ПОСЛЮ АГГЛЕ ЛА МОЕГО ПРЕ ЛИЦЕ ТВО
ИМЪ · И ОУГОТОВИТИ ПАТ ВОИ
ПРЕ ТОБОЮ · ГЛА ВОПІЮЩАГО ВПОУ
СТЫНИ · ОУГОТОВАИТЕ ПАГНЬ ·
ПРАВЫ СЪТВОРИТЕ СТЕЗА ЕГО ·
Ы КО А КРТА ВИ ЖСТЫНИ И ПРО
ПОВЪДАІА КРЩЕНІЕ ПОКАГАНІА ·
ВЪ ѠПАЩЩЕНІЕ ГРЪХО · ИС ХО
НЕ ПРЕПРОСКЪ · ЗАЛО ЕѴЛІА ·

OLD SLAVONIC, the predecessor of all

modern-day Slavic languages, was first codified in the citadel town of Nitra. The city and the land that is now Slovakia became the gateway of Christianity into the Slavic world. Tracing the footsteps of the two great Christian missionaries, Nitra is recognised by many as Eastern Europe's spiritual and cultural home.

This critical moment of opening the Slavs to the era of written language and the role Slovakia played in it, is eternally sealed in the modern Slovak language. Linguists refer to the language as the 'Esperanto of the East' taking us back to the time when Great Moravia became the gateway through which the Slavic alphabet entered the Slavic world.

Present day Slovakia is where the mother of all Slavic languages acquired its initial form. It was from this geographic nexus that the Slavic written language and therefore Slavic written knowledge first spread into Central and Eastern Europe. It is no surprise that modern Slovak shares a similar base with all modern Slavonic languages. Despite only being spoken by a population of 5.5 million people in Slovakia, the language is in fact the lingua franca of the Slavic East.

Try for yourself. Speak to any Slav in any Slav nation and hear their confirmation. Once you speak Slovak, you can find mutual understanding from Polish to Bulgarian, from Czech to Russian, from Croatian to Ukrainian. What is more, everyone across the Slavic world will understand the gentle little word 'Lipa'.

Constantine and Methodius understood that the past could not be done away with. They also recognized that the pagan beliefs of the Slavic people had a powerful hold over their emotions, thoughts and behaviours. The brothers were aware that if the Christian religion was to last past their departure. They had to find a way to achieve complete local devotion.

To reflect the taste of the times and make way for a new spiritual belief system, the mythology of the ancient Slavs was combined with Christian convention. Constantine and Methodius strategically replaced the myths of the old world with new Christian stories.

A compromise was made and the sacred Linden tree was informally recognized by the Church as a spiritually important icon. The symbolism was tied to the cult of the goddess and the female deity worship practised in the traditions of the region. The new religion very respectfully, but also very cleverly, continued to observe this powerful connection. The pagan goddess Lada, associated with the Linden, was smoothly merged with, and later replaced by the Virgin Mary.

The introduction of the new religion forever reversed the way of life in the Slavic heartland. It also sealed the fate of the Slavs for centuries to come. Once the people were fully converted, their land, hearts and minds became a firm part of Christian Europe, to which the Slovaks still belong today.

In the end, the efforts of Constantine and Methodius gave birth not only to Slavic writing and Christianity, but also to Slavic recorded history. It was only from this point onwards that Great Moravia and the Slavs could be written into the records of history.

With Christianity spreading across the mountains and into the plains of Eastern Europe, old Slavonic became the third European language of the Roman Catholic Church, after Greek and Latin. In Great Moravia, the Bible was written and mass was served in Slavonic, rather than in the usual Latin. This was unheard of at the time, and would only happen again much later, during the 16th century reformation movements sweeping through Europe.

In the heart of Europe, the cult of the goddess proved too strong to do away with. Just like the Linden Goddess Lada and Venus of Moravia before her, the Virgin Mary embodied many of the same values and attributes of her divine predecessors.

Today, the popularity of Virgin Mary is an illustration of how these ancient beliefs continue to influence modern-day Slovaks. The Virgin is the patron saint of Slovakia and the country's most beloved Christian icon. It is here that her cult inspires the largest following in Eastern Europe.

Many spiritual sites connected to Mary are found in nature. Unsurprisingly, her shrines are often flanked by Linden trees.

The Slovak love of the Virgin Mary is a reminder that neither Christianity, nor the later industrialisation and rapid modernization of the country, have disrupted the Slovak bond with nature and their pagan ancestry.

The heart of the Marian Cult takes us to the small town of Mariánka, located in a serene forest of the Small Carpathians on the outskirts of modern-day Bratislava. Surrounded by Linden trees, the oldest pilgrimage place in Slovakia was also the first site dedicated to the Madonna in the Kingdom of Hungary. Here, beggars, mercenaries, kings and queens would rub shoulder-to-shoulder in the hope of healing and solace. Even today, entering Mariánka is a deeply mystical experience. Protected by the Linden and graced by the Virgin, Mariánka welcomes pilgrims from all over the world who flock to the scared site in their thousands.

Pope John Paul II, the first and only Slavic Pope to lead the Roman Catholic Church, revered the Virgin. True to his Slavic roots, he sought out and celebrated the divine feminine. John Paul entrusted his life to the Virgin Mary and expressed his surrender in his apostolic motto 'Totus Tuus' (Totally Yours in Latin).

The Great Slavic Pope visited Slovakia three times after the collapse of communism; in 1990, in 1995 and in 2003. Some believe that his deep devotion to the Slovaks, a very small population of Christians in comparison to the much larger Catholic nations, was because Mother Mary was the patron saint of the country. Slovakia and the feminine face of God held a very special place in his heart.

through the tool of writing, also helped to catalyse the intellectual development of the region. History reveals that the first university of the Slavic world was located near the magnificent Devín Castle, not far from Bratislava.

Perched high up on the tops of the Small Carpathians and overlooking the Danube and Morava rivers, this remarkable landmark was once the cradle of enlightenment for the entire Slavic civilization.

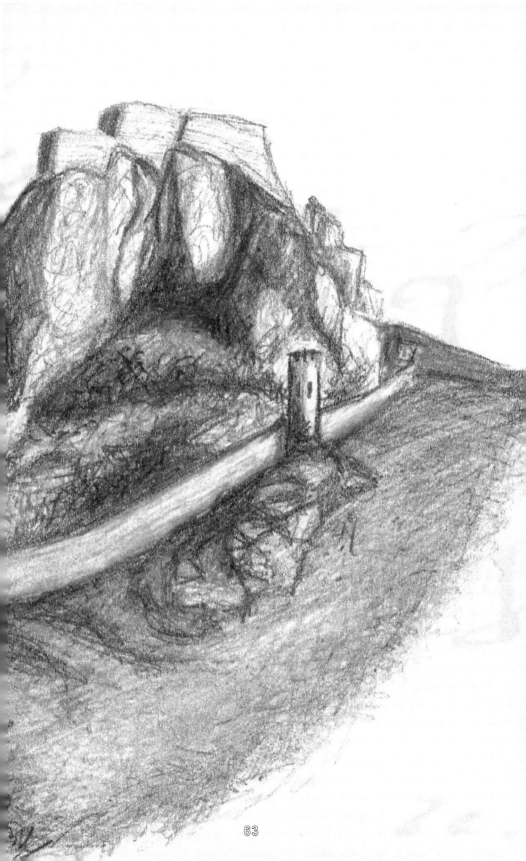

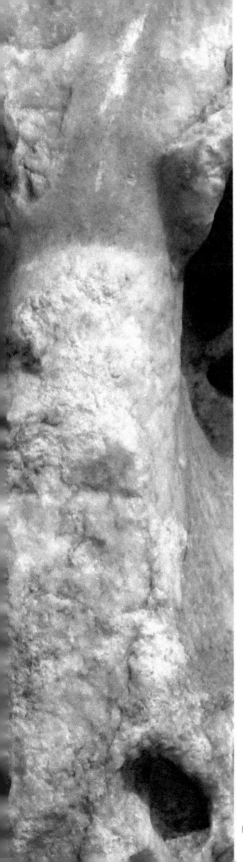

Under the tutorship of St. Constantine, the **head** and the soul of the University, a generation of Slavic scholars arose. They were shaped to go on and become international **emissaries** of the newly codified Slavic language, expanding the influence of Great Moravia throughout Europe and beyond.

As knowledge is power, its development very quickly spilled into the political prominence of Great Moravia. This did not go unnoticed by rival forces, the most **menacing** of these being the Frankish Empire. The Slavic kingdom was becoming an ever-greater thorn in their **eye**. A sword of Frankish revenge would soon be seen hanging above the heads of the Great Moravians.

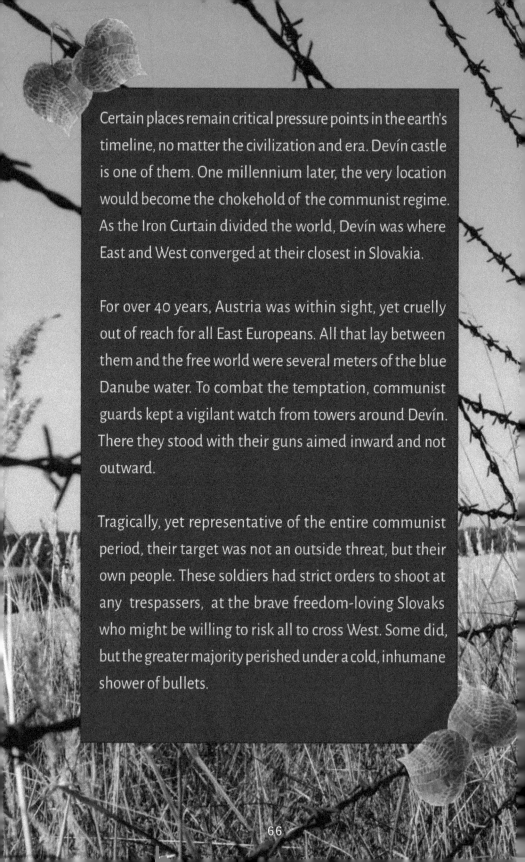

Certain places remain critical pressure points in the earth's timeline, no matter the civilization and era. Devín castle is one of them. One millennium later, the very location would become the chokehold of the communist regime. As the Iron Curtain divided the world, Devín was where East and West converged at their closest in Slovakia.

For over 40 years, Austria was within sight, yet cruelly out of reach for all East Europeans. All that lay between them and the free world were several meters of the blue Danube water. To combat the temptation, communist guards kept a vigilant watch from towers around Devín. There they stood with their guns aimed inward and not outward.

Tragically, yet representative of the entire communist period, their target was not an outside threat, but their own people. These soldiers had strict orders to shoot at any trespassers, at the brave freedom-loving Slovaks who might be willing to risk all to cross West. Some did, but the greater majority perished under a cold, inhumane shower of bullets.

V. IN THEIR END WAS THEIR BEGINNING

The price for settling in the den of European predators was soon to be paid. The harsh realities of medieval Europe could not be evaded. They crept up on the heart of Europe and its empire that had by now sprawled well beyond the boundaries of modern Slovakia.

The 9th century brought about much change to Europe as power was shifting. This was the time when the first glimpses of the end of the vast Frankish Empire arose when its ruler, the legendary Charlemagne, passed away. A formidable new force was brewing on their borders. The Vikings, a once removed threat, were about to set their sights on the power to be had on the continent. Meanwhile on the other side of Europe, the Byzantines were approaching their cultural and political climax.

Expanding Great Moravia was caught between worlds. Its growing strength and power was not to be tolerated as the kingdom stood in the way of the eclipsing Frankish Empire and its last desperate attempt to revive its dying glory.

Anxious to take control of the territory and supersede Byzantium, the Francs stormed into Great Moravia. But just like their greatest rivals, they understood that military aggression was not enough to secure dominance. They knew they had to win over the locals.

To break Byzantium's influence, the Franks had to end the **thought-leadership** of Slavic Europe. With the source of their knowledge gone, the power of the Slavs would wane too. In an act of **suppression**, the invaders ruthlessly burned the first Slavic university to the ground.

The mission was to do away with the new stronghold of Slavic wisdom and with the influence of St. Constantine and St. Methodius forever. As the seat of the Slavic power was removed, the Franks could become the sole source of **knowledge** for their civilization. The original Old Slavonic script was swiftly replaced with not only a new Latin alphabet, but a new way of **seeing** the world.

73

Shortly after the Franks enforced the implementation of the Emperor's Latin **alphabet,** they systematically pushed the original Slavonic script further and further East. Fortunately, not all was lost as the alphabet was able to survive and expand under the protection of the King of Bulgaria. Eventually, it would go on to give birth to the **Cyrillic script.**

To this day, Cyrillic is used by the nations to the east of Slovakia: the Russians, Bulgarians, Belarusians, Ukrainians, Serbians and Montenegrins. On the other hand, the lasting **imprint** of the 9th century Frank invasion and Latinization is sealed in every single word written in Slovak, Czech, Polish, Slovenian and Croatian. The countries still use the **Latin** alphabet today.

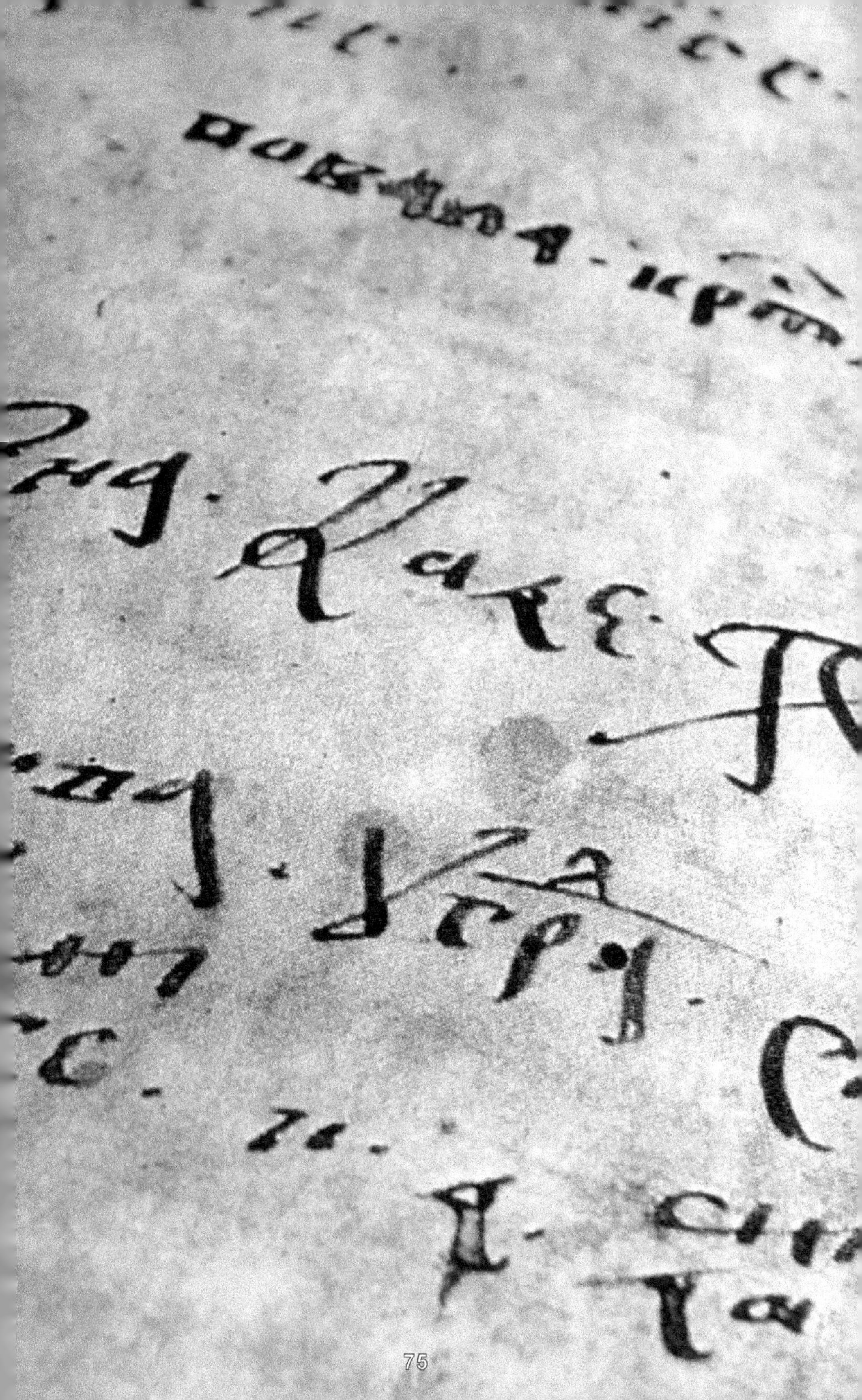

The turn of the 1st millennium witnessed not only the fall of **Great Moravia**, but also the forgetting of its legacy in Europe. The Kingdom of the Slavs is still a mystery to us. Yet these events not only ended one era, but also sowed the seeds for a new future.

The fall of Great Moravia marked the beginning of a region opening to an ever-greater Europe. However devastating, the Frankish invasion was just the beginning of a thorny path ahead.

VI. NESTED IN THE HUNGARIAN HEARTLAND

Destabilised

Destabilised by the Franks, the people were

disoriented and left to their own devices when the nomadic warriors from the East came. These newcomers would forever change Europe and the fate of the people underneath the Tatras. Their lands were gradually swallowed-up by the growing kingdom of the Magyars.

Just like the Slavs, the origins of the old Magyars continue to baffle experts. It is believed that they came from somewhere in Asia. The fertile plain in the centre of Europe seduced them to break with their nomadic tradition. Unexpectedly, the Magyars decided to put down their roots and settle for good in and around the heart of Europe.

THAT
SINGLE
DECISION

changed the region. Firmly rooted on the continent, the Magyars swiftly accelerated their ambitions over the territory into what would become a remarkable thousand-year reign.

Contrary to their reputation for being oppressive and authoritarian, the early Hungarian kings set out with the intention to build an inclusive kingdom. They opened the territory to varied influences, including those of the Slavs. The new rulers sourced experts, scholars and artists from across the continent and beyond to build a powerful state. Many cultural exchanges, including inter-tribal marriages, ensued.

THE MAGYAR OVERLORDS

were open to learning and embracing the symbolism of the conquered people. It was no different with the Linden tree. One of the most illustrious and successful kings, Matthias Corvinus, planted a Lipa in the park of one of his favourite castle estates. Observing the Slavic tradition, this is where royal assemblies were held. The regal Linden tree sent an important message to the people of the region that their heritage and their identity were respected. Seven hundred years later, the same tree is still stretching its thick crown against the sky in Bojnice Castle.

The **northern neighbours** from the former Great Moravia had much to share with the newcomers. Their long tradition and experience in agriculture was a skill that the nomadic Magyars had not yet developed. Who else to draw this **wisdom** from than those intimately connected with the local land for centuries before their arrival? A wave of learning followed which left a **lasting imprint** on the Hungarian language. Vocabulary devoted to agriculture bore a distinct resemblance to Slovak.

Yet, as time went on, the ambitions of the Magyar rulers grew, mirroring the imperial tastes of European superpowers of the day. Competition for power and influence was rife in the condensed space of Europe.

Hungarian aspirations were temporarily crushed by an **Ottoman occupation** beginning in 1526, lasting over 150 years. The oriental influence reached as far north as Slovakia. Yet, its mountains offered a refuge for the Hungarian civilization and soon **Bratislava** became the capital city of the Hungarian Kingdom.

In addition to being drained by the **conquests** of the sultans from the East, the Hungarian kingdom had to face the stubborn Habsburgs. The **dynasty** presiding over the Empire of Austria felt predestined to rule over the region.

Despite aggression from the East followed by manipulation from the West, it was not in the blood of the warrior nation to give up without a fight. Eventually a concession was made and a new strategic alliance was cultivated. Hungary emerged as a partner to the Austrians in a dual monarchy.

In retrospect, the establishment of **Austria-Hungary** was a historic moment in Europe's history, but it was also symbolic of a half-hearted attempt at modernisation and compromise. Behind the façade of equality, the Austrians continued to dominate the alliance militarily, administratively, politically and culturally. This **fanned the flames** of the Hungarian frustration. It also drove them to seek their political and cultural dominance in other parts of the monarchy, over much smaller and defenceless nations.

As the wheel of evolution moved towards the 19th century Austria-Hungary found itself stagnating as it oscillated between the medieval **feudal kingdom** of its past and a modern state. The empire was struggling to take a decisive step forward.

The Monarchy was a composite of paradoxes. It was still one of the most liberal of the last three standing empires in Europe. The progressive way of life in Austria-Hungary made the Romanovs and Ottomans look archaic in comparison.

Life within Austria-Hungary brought Slovaks many advantages. These included military protection, trade infrastructure, modernisation of education, public administration and a high European culture. At the same time, the monarchy, especially towards its end, became synonymous with imperial indifference, class arrogance and cultural oppression.

Slovakia was greatly enriched by being part of the multi-ethnic imperium. Bratislava's prominent location on the Danube, Europe's second longest river, and between the two capitals, Vienna and Budapest, gave the country exposure to extensive trade routes.

The Silk Road, which dates back to the 2nd century, was an ancient trade network that connected China with the Mediterranean and beyond. It was much more than an economic bloodline. The Road bridged diverging worlds, peoples, cultures, goods and ideas. Exotic foods, spices and artefacts from faraway lands were sold and exchanged along the trail, changing European needs and wants forever. It was the Silk Road that first ignited Europe's love affair with the Orient.

The Amber Road which represented the North to South trade connection also crossed through Slovakia. Merchants travelled from the Baltic Sea to the Mediterranean and further into Africa transporting and trading highly sought-after amber. The now lost Amber room which was once proclaimed the 8th wonder of the world is one of the greatest reminders of the bygone epoch, hallmarked by its precious fossilised resin.

The Silk Road and the Amber Road crossed in present day Bratislava. The trade elites not only brought produce to Slovakia, they also took Slovak produce to the world, among them artefacts carved from Linden wood. In turn, the essence of what makes up Slovak identity reached the far corners of the world.

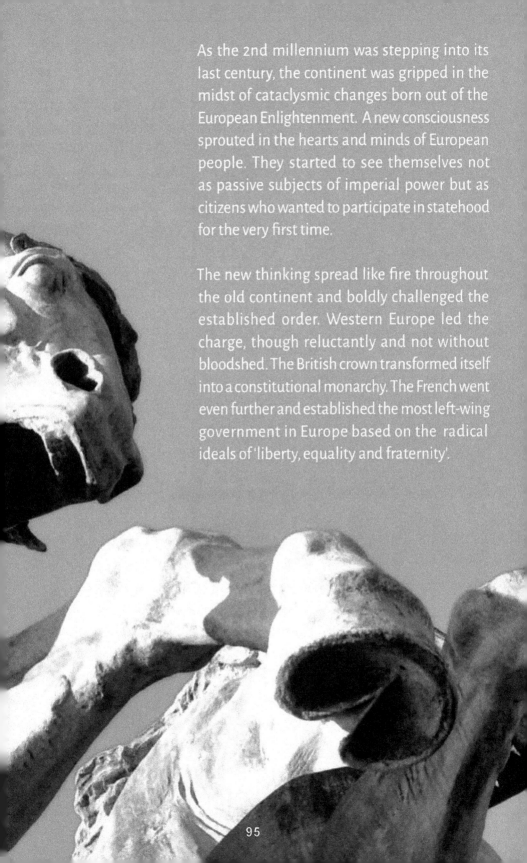

As the 2nd millennium was stepping into its last century, the continent was gripped in the midst of cataclysmic changes born out of the European Enlightenment. A new consciousness sprouted in the hearts and minds of European people. They started to see themselves not as passive subjects of imperial power but as citizens who wanted to participate in statehood for the very first time.

The new thinking spread like fire throughout the old continent and boldly challenged the established order. Western Europe led the charge, though reluctantly and not without bloodshed. The British crown transformed itself into a constitutional monarchy. The French went even further and established the most left-wing government in Europe based on the radical ideals of 'liberty, equality and fraternity'.

Austria-Hungary trailed behind the new trend. In many ways, the monarchy in the heart of the continent was a relic of the old Europe, one which no longer existed. It was ruled by an obstinate emperor clinging on to traditional values that no longer reflected the dynamism of a changed world. Sabotaged by the emperor's blind quest for absolute power and continuous belittlement of his co-ruling Magyars, the empire weakened from within. The monarchy showed few signs of willingness to adapt as it tip-toed on the verge of collapse.

Determined to not succumb to Habsburg pressure and to catch up with the forward-thinking Europe, the Hungarians decided to unify their part of the empire at all costs, as a matter of survival. To preserve their power against the calls for greater freedom coming from all corners and peoples, they were prepared to do anything. They were even ready to wipe out its ethnic diversity by erasing the memories, cultures and languages of the people who inhabited the land under the dominion of the kingdom.

This led to the implementation of the infamous magyarisation policies, that carried the slogan 'one state, one nation, one language' at their core. To some, they were an attempt to modernise the kingdom and harmonize the chaos of the diverse monarchy, then speaking thirteen languages. To others, it was an act of savage tyranny.

Decades of cultural colonization across the kingdom ensued. All legal, institutional and formal correspondence was to be conducted only in Hungarian. All inhabitants of the kingdom, regardless of their cultural and ethnic background, were to be educated only in Hungarian.

SLOVAKIA

SLOVAKIA, then known as Upper Hungary, once again paid the price of being located at the crossroads of worlds. It did not escape the cruelty of the Hungarian assimilation policies. This is where magyarisation was at its harshest. Why? The province with its centre in Bratislava, or Pozsony to the Hungarians, was not to be lost. After all, it had been the capital of the Hungarian kingdom during the years of the Ottoman occupation.

Mountainous Slovakia was also critical to the defence of the Hungarian flat heartland. The consequences reached into the daily lives of the Slovaks. If a Slovak aspired to be more than a farm hand, he or she had to adapt and assimilate into the Hungarian mindset. Speaking in Hungarian and behaving like a Hungarian was indispensable to all career development and, of course, to any upward social mobility.

D istinctive cultural allegiances, such as speaking one's mother tongue and practising one's folklore, carried a very serious political danger. Identifying oneself as Slovak came at a great risk for people who were mostly humble peasants. Disobedience could, and did, cost them their lives.

The omnipresent Lipa, the symbol of Slavdom, had no place in the Magyar vision. The cultural icon of the Linden tree was forgotten as all things Slovak were strategically and systematically devalued to make way for the rise of a single Hungarian nation. This was done with meticulous precision, a customary practice of colonizers to subvert or destroy symbols revered by the locals.

As the old world was crumbling around Austria-Hungary in the run-up to the first ever global conflict in human history, Slovak culture too was collapsing under the brutal oppression of magyarization. Just a step away from annihilation, the Slovak people miraculously rose to save their language and culture.

The Slovak National Awakening came as a surge of resistance movements swept through the monarchy. From across the empire, a collective of voices emerged demanding cultural rights and freedoms. By then, the people had enough of the oppression. They wanted control over their children's future and a say in their nation's destiny.

T ransition did not come easy. The elites were exasperated at having their authority challenged after six centuries of Habsburg rule and almost a millennium by the Kingdom of Hungary. The idea of sharing power was fiercely resisted by both Austrians and Hungarians.

The discord between the power players and those demanding their sovereignty spiralled into a series of insurgencies. Blood was shed across the old empire. Every battle became a lesson learned, just as every act of defiance became a step towards the establishment of an autonomous Slovak nation.

None other than the Lipa was resurrected as the silent symbol of the great awakening of the Slovak Slavs. No matter how hard the Hungarian rulers tried to remove it from the public memory, the sacred tree was too deeply rooted in the nation. It became the emblem for a united Slavic identity, that could not be suppressed forever.

THE LINDEN

became the secret code of the Slovak and Slavic resistance and the inspiration behind a vision of the Slovak nation. It emboldened the hearts and the minds of Slovakia's founding fathers, who bravely embarked on an unthinkable mission.

In a battle pitching David against Goliath, Slovaks bravely faced the Hungarian power apparatus to give Slovaks the right to be Slovak.

Their effort was driven by the tiny Slovak intelligentsia who understood that the rise of the Slovak nation was dependent on having its own language.

It is astonishing to think that old Slavonic was codified in the 9th century, while modern Slovak had to wait until 1843. As the 19th century gave way to a new era, Slovaks rose proud and tall, just like their mighty national tree, to take a stand for sovereignty and justice. They quickly codified their language and used it to advocate for their national rights.

THE SLOVAK NATIONAL AWAKENING

was successful despite being championed by a very small group of passionate Slovaks. This is because it was driven by a love for Slovakia, rather than hate towards the Hungarians. It was love that brought Slovaks together to commit an unthinkable act of bravery. The iconic Lipa code, the symbol of love represented their mission.

Ironically, it was the uncompromising magyarisation policies that awakened their uncompromising love for their own culture and language. However, they would have to wait until the First World War brought about the end of the empire and gave Slovaks their first taste of sovereignty.

Had the Magyars been more embracing of the cultural diversity of their kingdom, we might be living in a very different Europe. We will never know. What we know for certain is that the Slovaks never forgot what happened to them.

THE DISTRUST of the Hungarians still

runs in the veins of Slovaks . It is little known outside the region that Slovaks never refer to the empire as that of Austria-Hungary due to this painful history.

When speaking about the dual monarchy, Slovaks call it Rakúsko - Uhorsko (Austria-Uhorsko), rather than Rakúsko - Maďarsko' (Austria-Hungary). According to Slovaks, Maďarsko is the name for modern Hungary, while Uhorsko refers to an ancient kingdom they were once a part of.

The empire was a conglomerate of 20 different ethnic groups and 13 different languages. The greatness of the Uhorsko kingdom was in its diversity. From food to folklore and from knowledge to resources it enriched the European civilization. However, when mismanaged, this cauldron of diversity also proved to be its greatest weakness.

VIII. CZECHOSLOVAKIA: THE SLAVIC DREAM TEAM

The end of the First World War saw one of the oldest European empires fall on its knees. Destabilised by internal tensions and overpowered by the Western allied forces, Austria-Hungary lost not only the war, but almost everything it once owned.

The Trianon Treaty, still remembered as the Trianon betrayal by the Hungarians, saw 67% of Hungarian lands and 60% of the Hungarian population taken away to form new nations. The dissolution of the empire secured their long-awaited freedom.

The post-war arrangements created a new country born out of a much older bond. The unification of the Czechs and Slovaks awakened long forgotten memories of a shared history going back one millennium. Czechoslovakia was built on the foundations of the bygone Great Moravia.

1938

THE UNION of the two kin nations also embodied the best of the masculine and feminine aspects of Slavic expression. The combination of Czech intellect and Slovak emotion gave birth to a powerful alliance whose short-lived legacy, much like that of Great Moravia, was equal to the greatest of legends.

ČESKOSLOVENSKO

1918   1938

2 Kč   2 Kč

CZECHOSLOVAKIA

would go on to become one of Europe's and the world's most progressive and industrially advanced countries. To seal and celebrate the new union, a symbol dating back to Great Moravia was chosen. It was to become the visual embodiment of the new country on the map of Europe.

The Linden tree and its heart-shaped leaf reached deep into the roots of both cultures. The tree, long ago referred to as a microcosm of the universe and bridge between worlds, strengthened the cultural and spiritual ties between the brethren nations. The Lipa tradition has not been shaken since as the Linden remains the national tree of both the Czech Republic and Slovakia today.

Sadly, the Bohemian **enchantment** was not immune to the destiny of a region situated on the crossroads of civilizations. **Post-war** destabilization gave rise to new power struggles. Once again, foreign influences were ready to disrupt the peace in the heart of the old continent.

The warning signs of yet another **global conflict** were at first ignored by many. Europe closed its eyes to the rise of the Third Reich on the doorstep of Czechoslovakia. The young country and her people would pay dearly. Strategically positioned and industrially sophisticated, Czechoslovakia was critical to **Hitler's** master plan for global **domination.**

The Czech lands became part of Hitler's protectorate and Slovakia a Nazi satellite state. The war and fascism left a deep scar on both countries and Slovakia's Jewish population was almost completely wiped amid public passivity. However, the Slovaks eventually rose against the tyranny. Their courageous effort marked the second biggest rebellion against Nazi Germany in Europe. The event entered history as the Slovak National Uprising.

made a grave mistake when Hitler came knocking at their door. In an effort to prevent another war from breaking out just twenty years after the devastating WWI, the Munich agreement saw the major powers of Europe abandon the great Slavic republic in an act of appeasement. With their cowardly approval, Czechoslovakia was conceded to the Nazis without Czechoslovak representatives even being invited to talks.

Immediately, the Czech lands were annexed and a puppet state under the control of Hitler was declared in Slovakia. To this day, bitterness runs in the veins of Slovaks who remember it as the **kiss of Judas** from those whom they trusted. The Munich Treaty is a Munich Betrayal to them.

The German occupiers mastered mass fear, terror and mind control. It did not take long for them to grasp the significance of the local Linden symbolism and exploit it to promote their interests. During the Second World War, the Linden leaf was strategically weaponized to fortify German domination over the invaded country.

With the Czech part of the country occupied and Slovakia under the watchful eye of the Germans, the Czechoslovak leadership in exile found a haven in London. Here, Slovaks and Czechs, who refused to accept the fate forced upon them by the Nazi suzerain, plotted to reclaim their country.

It was in London that the event that marked the turning point of the Second World War was orchestrated under the code name 'Operation Anthropoid'. The plan was to assassinate Reinhard Heydrich, Hitler's right hand and the architect of the Holocaust.

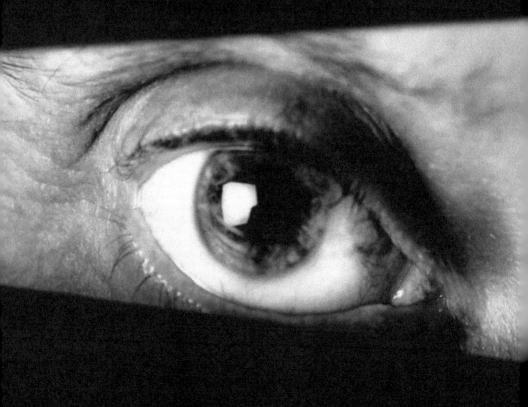

The British-trained Czechoslovak soldiers were successful in executing the mission, surrendering their own lives. Only then the West realised that the atrocities of Hitler could no longer be ignored and the Munich Treaty was declared null and void. Europe and the allied forces entered a fully-fledged war against Nazi Germany.

Poignantly, the London headquarters of the Czechoslovak government in exile bore the name Villa Lipa, so strong was their mutual affiliation to the sacred tree of their ancestors. It was no surprise that Anthropoid, one of the most heroic acts in the history of Czechoslovakia, Europe and the world, was adorned with the power of the ancient symbol.

IX. DRAWING THE IRON CURTAIN

Nothing lasts forever and the even the seemingly unending tragedy that saw over 60 million souls perish came to an end. In the aftermath of a Europe shattered by the greatest war ever to have affected the planet, Czechoslovakia was reunited and revived once again.

The post-war jubilation was to last only a few years. As the country sought to re-orientate itself and begin to re-build what was damaged, a new dividing line across Europe was drawn. It would take the form of a cold and impenetrable political barrier.

With Czechoslovakia located in the dead centre on the East-West geopolitical frontline, the country was absorbed into the Soviet sphere of control. Yet, at the time, the Soviets were revered in Slavic Europe as the liberators from the Nazi terror. It was natural that organic alliances based on a common Slavic identity formed between the Soviet and Czechoslovak people.

Speaking a similar language, the Russians were esteemed as cousins. This closeness quickly escalated into social and political entanglements. A friendly camaraderie between the Slavic cousins was not enough. The leaders of the Soviet Union had much bolder ambitions in mind and they did not stop short of using the power of the Linden symbol to achieve them.

Eager to implement its vision,

Moscow organized a coup that brought an end to renewed democracy in the heart of Europe. Just three years into post-war peace, the forceful takeover of Czechoslovakia set the precedent for Soviet domination of the region which would continue until almost the end of the 20th century

The Linden became a useful token in the eyes of the Soviets. Not only did it celebrate the Slavic essence, it also glorified inter-Slav closeness. The symbol quickly merged with pro-communist propaganda to pull on Czechoslovak heartstrings in order to reduce their self-identification with the capitalist West.

Weakened by the loss of population and travesties of the Second World War, the Czechoslovak people's actions and views were navigated by a survival mentality. They proved willing to give their power away in return for any sign of security and stability. The new Soviet regime recognised this need, or weakness, and used it to entrench itself in power.

Decades of show trials, purges, mass relocations, censorship and pervasive surveillance reached into the innermost lives of the citizens of Czechoslovakia. The objective of this Moscow-instigated strategy was straightforward and simple: a nation kept disoriented, abused and, above all, fearful, was easy to control.

The reality of the Soviet transition was not all doom and gloom as is often portrayed. The Soviets also brought hope to many with their new ideology. Despite the interwar interlude of democracy in Czechoslovakia, the thousand year-long imperial rule and abuse were still fresh memories.

The Empire of Austria-Hungary was built on an exploitative feudal system that made serfs hand over their free labour to the land-owning nobility. In exchange, they were allowed to live on the land, but were never paid money. Their effort was never recognized. This system not only flattened their spirit, it also perpetuated a class hierarchy while allowing no means to escape dire poverty.

COMMUNISM

offered a radical alternative. It was a new vision based on egalitarian values and justice, where no man was better or worse than his brethren. The ideology also provided an answer to the betrayal of Czechoslovakia in the Munich Treaty. According to Moscow, the West was never to be trusted again.

More importantly, communism was enticing because the message came from a fellow Slavic people. Communism reflected the innate collective ideals of the Slavic nations. It also carried many of the egalitarian tribal values of their shared ancient pagan ancestors.

DESPITE THE ALLURE

of sweet promises of escaping the pain of the past, Slovaks remained vigilant. The nation that had gone through unimaginable abuse throughout history did not trust easily.

While the communists were popular among the Czechs and were even democratically elected into power before the coup, their support in Slovakia was much weaker. The sensitive Slovak radar, fine-tuned by centuries of social, cultural, military and political catastrophes proved to be very accurate.

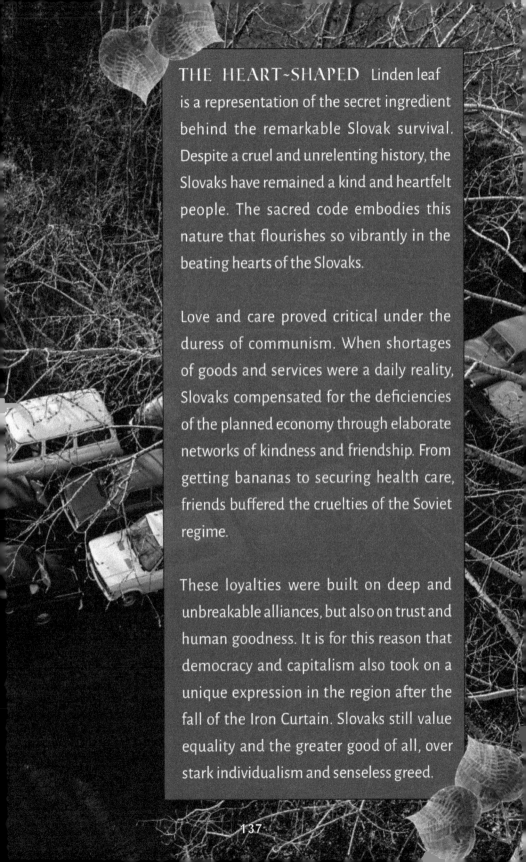

THE HEART-SHAPED Linden leaf is a representation of the secret ingredient behind the remarkable Slovak survival. Despite a cruel and unrelenting history, the Slovaks have remained a kind and heartfelt people. The sacred code embodies this nature that flourishes so vibrantly in the beating hearts of the Slovaks.

Love and care proved critical under the duress of communism. When shortages of goods and services were a daily reality, Slovaks compensated for the deficiencies of the planned economy through elaborate networks of kindness and friendship. From getting bananas to securing health care, friends buffered the cruelties of the Soviet regime.

These loyalties were built on deep and unbreakable alliances, but also on trust and human goodness. It is for this reason that democracy and capitalism also took on a unique expression in the region after the fall of the Iron Curtain. Slovaks still value equality and the greater good of all, over stark individualism and senseless greed.

X. THE FRAGRANT PRAGUE SPRING AND ITS BRUTAL SUPPRESSION

Twenty years into the imposed orthodoxy of the totalitarian regime, a spark of hope spontaneously ignited in the hearts of the Czechoslovaks. Helped by the generation exchange, a new light emerged unexpectedly to expose the darkness of Soviet-controlled Europe.

Young people coming of age could no longer be held captive by the same fears and power manoeuvres that stripped the will of their parents. Their desire for a better and freer life proved too great to be denied. Hand in hand with the changed outlook of the people came a relaxation of the regime.

In the 1960s, it was no longer unthinkable to criticise those in power and it became easier to travel abroad. Slowly but surely, the country began opening its borders to the world.

As time went by, little freedoms eventually escalated into an overall demand for greater national autonomy. The Prague Spring arrived. Just like the sprouting seedling of the sacred Linden tree, Czechoslovakia was ready to pierce through the soil and stretch its branches beyond the confines of it's national borders.

'Socialism with a human face',

championed by Alexander Dubček, a much beloved Slovak,

became the slogan of the era. The revolution was well underway and the sweet promise of liberty, inspired by the Prague Spring, could almost be tasted. It was as luscious as the rich fragrance of blooming Lindens in that iconic and unforgettable summer of 1968.

Unfortunately,

the passion, vision and hope of a maturing Czechoslovakia was too advanced for the times. The prospect of losing the country to liberty was too great a threat to the Soviet Union. Moscow was determined to keep Czechoslovakia at all costs. The events that followed spoke volumes of just how important the country at the doorstep of the West was to their political and military interests.

As the peaceful revolution blossomed, Moscow acted swiftly. On the night of the 20th of August, a joint Warsaw Pact army of 500,000 soldiers crossed the border of Czechoslovakia marking the beginning of an invasion. All hope of freedom came crashing down when Soviet tanks rolled into the streets of Prague and Bratislava.

sent by Moscow delivered a clear message. The Soviet Union was here to stay and it was not to be messed with. The military occupation of the country, that would last for the next two decades, was immediately followed by a succession of changes.

The liberal Dubček was removed. His visionary ideals were replaced by a man whose mind matched that of the Party hardliners. Gustáv Husák went on to become the new uncompromising leader marshalling the Soviet agenda.

Moscow's puppet or parrot, as some would call him, followed orders to the tee. He implemented 'normalisation' with ruthless efficiency. This began a long and cruel period of systematic suppression when the imprisonment not just of Czechoslovak bodies but also their minds was commonplace.

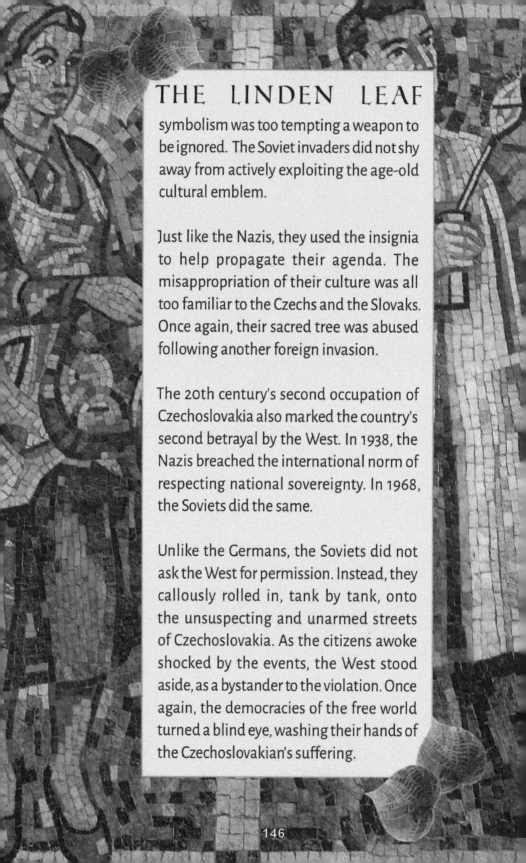

THE LINDEN LEAF

symbolism was too tempting a weapon to be ignored. The Soviet invaders did not shy away from actively exploiting the age-old cultural emblem.

Just like the Nazis, they used the insignia to help propagate their agenda. The misappropriation of their culture was all too familiar to the Czechs and the Slovaks. Once again, their sacred tree was abused following another foreign invasion.

The 20th century's second occupation of Czechoslovakia also marked the country's second betrayal by the West. In 1938, the Nazis breached the international norm of respecting national sovereignty. In 1968, the Soviets did the same.

Unlike the Germans, the Soviets did not ask the West for permission. Instead, they callously rolled in, tank by tank, onto the unsuspecting and unarmed streets of Czechoslovakia. As the citizens awoke shocked by the events, the West stood aside, as a bystander to the violation. Once again, the democracies of the free world turned a blind eye, washing their hands of the Czechoslovakian's suffering.

XI. TRANSITION YEARS: THE NOT SO 'VELVET' 90S

It would take another **20 years** and another generation exchange before Czechoslovakia would breathe freely again. In November 1989, the Iron Curtain finally came tumbling down in what became known as the Velvet Revolution. It was a **peaceful movement** that brought down four decades of communist dictatorship in Eastern Europe.

The shift from totalitarian control to democracy and free market was radical. As the old-world order of the Soviet bloc collapsed in the heart of the continent, so did Czechoslovakia. The **Velvet Divorce** came suddenly. There was no referendum to reflect the will of the people. Instead, the decision was made unexpectedly by the political elites of the time. With no great preparation or **ceremony,** the brethren Czechs and Slovaks parted ways in silence.

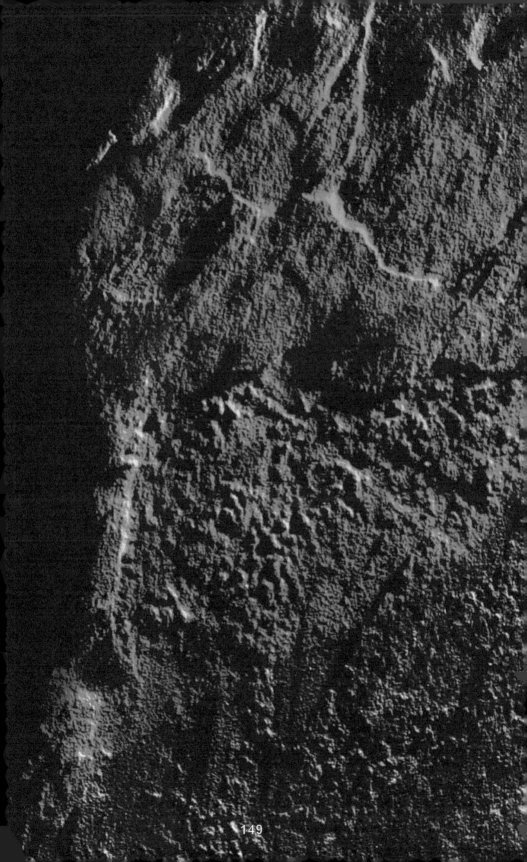

The monumental changes brought great insecurity and **instability** to the people and the country. Although the ousting of communism was welcomed, the transition from absolute state control to a whole new ideology of democracy proved thorny and difficult. **Communist** thinking infused the public and the private lives of the people for multiple generations.

The state had **controlled** not only what they could talk and read about, but also what they could own, what they could learn, and worst of all, what they could think. Almost overnight, it was over and there was great pressure to **adjust** and catch up with the ways of the West. It was overwhelming.

In a **whirlwind of confusion,** Slovaks struggled to situate themselves. Great psychological disturbances left scars on many lives as everything the people had been taught to believe as 'truth' was exposed as a fraud, a mere power gimmick by their totalitarian controllers.

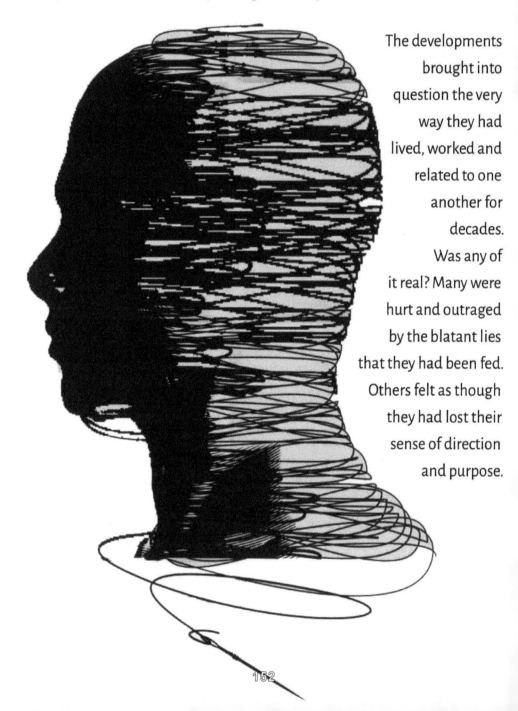

The developments brought into question the very way they had lived, worked and related to one another for decades. Was any of it real? Many were hurt and outraged by the blatant lies that they had been fed. Others felt as though they had lost their sense of direction and purpose.

Some even became nostalgic for the old and familiar world of the authoritarian, but paternal communists. The safety and security that communism provided in exchange for absolute obedience was in a stark contrast to the wavering uncertainty of the transitional years.

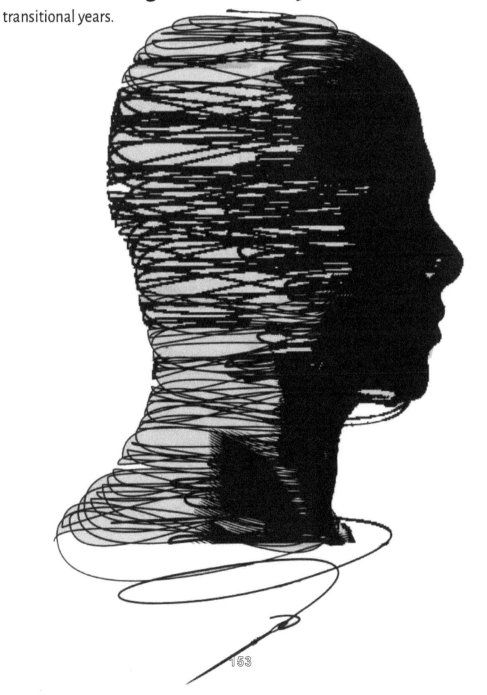

As with any great and unexpected transition,

when the old is made obsolete and the new is not yet formed, a vacuum emerges as it did in Slovakia. Violence, kidnappings, thefts, murders and cronyism plagued the recovering society for much of the decade.

A wild west style of capitalism took over the country, where the state and a select few gained access to the country's wealth through privatization. With no money and no vision, the people began to lose hope for a better future.

As enthusiasm for democracy was waning, apathy took over. The future looked bleak and not even the force of the Linden code could help.

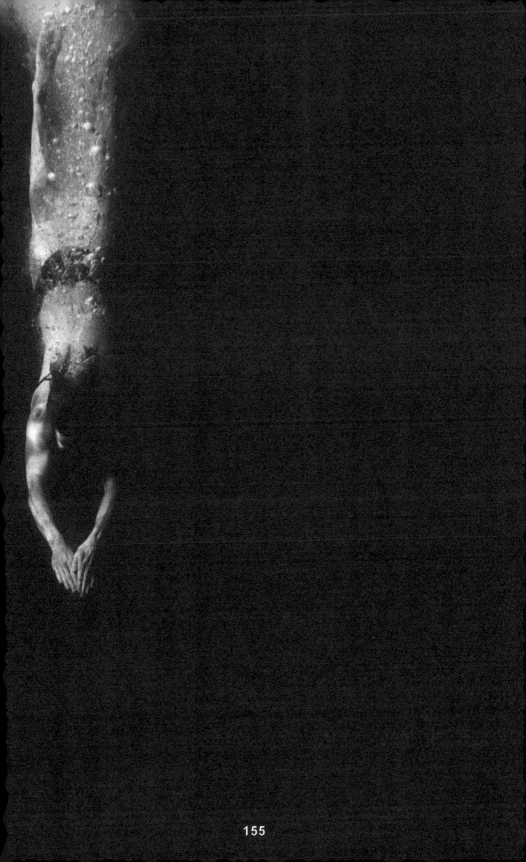

IT WAS AT THIS CRITICAL POINT

in their history that the true spirit of the Slovaks resurfaced.

No longer a controlled and exploited nation, the Slovaks had to stop being victims and start seeing themselves as a sovereign people responsible for the good of their country.

For the first time in history, they were to blame for their own difficulties. Forced to look long and hard in the mirror, Slovaks had to admit to their own wrongdoing before they could make way for a change.

Above all, the Slovaks' love for the Lipa was far too great. The attempt to hijack the precious code to push dangerous political and personal interests was a step too far by Vladimír Mečiar, the most controversial public figure in recent Slovak history. Once celebrated as the father of the newly sovereign Slovakia, his power-hungry ways soon led him astray. Mečiar was prepared to do anything to keep and expand his influence in the country.

In a desperate attempt to defy a call for change, he employed the powerful Linden code in the run up to the 1998 elections. His party handed out Linden seeds at meet and greets in the hope of swaying voters. But the Slovaks would not tolerate the abuse of the sacred tree again. Mečiar was defeated.

XII. THE SLOVAK PHOENIX EMERGES

The turbulent 1990s are a painful chapter in the history of the freshly independent nation. Slovakia became internationally known as the black hole at the heart of Europe. The memorable words spoken by Madeleine Albright, the US secretary of State, herself a Czechoslovak emigrant, summed up the emptiness and despair that many people felt.

Sometimes in life, we have to hit the rock bottom before we can rise again. This could not have been any truer for the people of the heart of Europe. At the height of the greatest turmoil a phoenix from behind the shadows defiantly emerged. The Slovaks decided to take ownership of their destiny. With this profound shift in thinking came an equally profound break with the past. At long last, they were independent and free, but the lessons of the 1990s showed them that with freedom also came responsibility.

THE Slovaks rose from the ashes and set sail into the third millennium in a turnaround that few ever thought possible. Diligence and perseverance bred into the Slovaks by the perils of their existence on the crossroads came to fruition in the most meticulous of fashions.

In a remarkably brief time, Slovakia embraced the world and successfully transitioned from communism to democracy and from cronyism to a dynamic and well-functioning economy. Even more importantly, the nation transformed itself from being the object to being the subject of its own history.

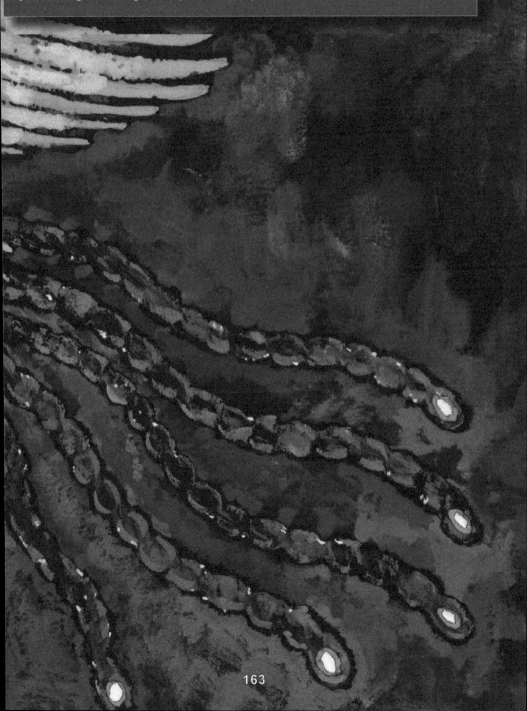

SLOVAKIA and her people had grown tired of others writing their stories. As the second millennium came to a close, the world watched in amazement as the brave Slovak phoenix, the spirit of the people, finally spread its giant wings on top of the leafy crown of the Lipa tree.

XIII.   HIDDEN IN PLAIN SIGHT

The heart-shaped leaf of the beloved tree is deeply entwined with the daily reality of modern Slovakia. It is so common that it might be unseen to the naked eye, but all you need to do is pay attention to the world around you. It will not take long to discover that the Linden follows you at each and every step you make in Slovakia.

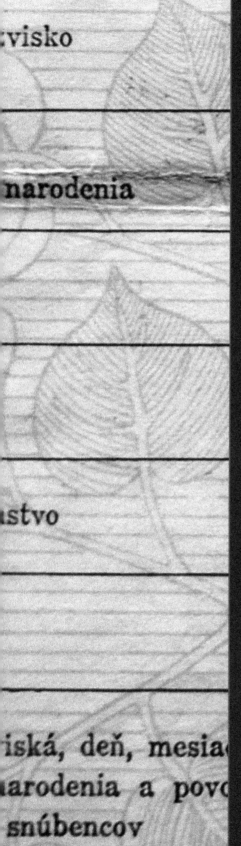

THE SYMBOL

can be found across the social, civic and even political life of the country. The Linden code is omnipresent. At the very top, it adorns the national seal of Slovakia and has its firm place on the coat of arms of the President. It also enlivens the institutional imagery of Slovak ministries, cities and villages, as well as the country's universities and theatres.

The Linden tree and symbol penetrate literature, folklore and architecture. It is everywhere, from the postal stamps reaching the furthest corners of the world, to the most practical expression of modern citizenship. The iconic Lipa leaf marks Slovak passports and national identity cards. Slovaks carry their sacred code with them everywhere and every day.

The sweet and gentle tea brewed from delicate Linden flowers is the signature drink of the Slovak nation. It warms the hearts of Slovaks of all ages. It is the drink they reach for when they seek comfort and relaxation.

166

Ústredn...

Prvý výpis, bez poplatku.

SOBÁŠNY LIST

V KNIHE M...ŽELSTIEV   ústredného   NÁRODNEHO VÝBORU

v   Bratislave

STRANE 91 POD ČISLOM RADOVÝM 840 ROKU

YO SVÄZKU ...   STRANE ... JE ZAPISANE ...edentisícdev...

	21.6.1952/ dvads... desi...
Deň, mesiac, rok a miesto uzavretia manželstva	ženích
Meno a priezvisko	Ľudevít Izák 1C. augusta 1... Trenčín
Deň, mesiac, rok a miesto narodenia	slobodný
Stav	úradník
Povolanie	Čs.
Štátna občianstvo	Bra...
Bydlisko	ne... 8...
Mená a priezviská, deň, mesiac, rok, miesto narodenia a povolanie rodičov	
Mená a priezviská, povolanie a bydlisko svedkov	
Poznámky	

Bratislave   dňa 2. júla 1952...

THE INSIGNIA

THE INSIGNIA expands far beyond mere material imagery. The heart-shaped leaf carves its trail in the emotional tapestry of the culture and the people. It is a living connection between the ancient world of the Slavs and modern Slovakia. From artistic expression, to the spiritual realm, the Linden is encoded in the Slovak DNA.

Going back to the Christianisation of the Slavs, Lipa seedlings were planted next to newly erected religious structures in the hope of converting the locals. The tradition continues uninterrupted today. From the west to the east and the north to the south, the outstretched branches of tall and beautiful Linden trees, some centuries old, can be seen swaying in the breeze next to churches, chapels and shrines throughout the country. The intimacy and charm of their presence is truly a sight to behold.

DIVING DEEPER,

the Lipa eulogy stretches into the Slavic mysticism that Slovaks still keep alive. The tree symbolised the cycle of life to their ancient predecessors. It commemorated the entry and departure of the human soul from this world into the next.

Today, the sprouting, blossoming, withering and finally barren tree reminds Slovaks of the delicate balance of life. Which is why they still plant a Linden tree on the occasion of a child's birth.

On the other end of the human life cycle, the Lipa brings solace to those in grief. Cemeteries are often blessed with the presence of mature Linden trees whispering words of comfort and casting their protection over departed loved ones.

CONCLUSION

SLOVAKS:
A PEOPLE OF THE HEART

It is symbolic that the nation of the heart-shaped leaf also lies in the very heart of Europe. The dividing lines of the continent have never failed to run through the country, exposing Slovaks to competing worldviews that have swept through Europe and bringing destruction of the old and rise of the new.

From the Pagan old to the Christian new, from the Orthodox East to the Latin West, from the empires of the past to Slavic sovereignty, from communism to democracy, Slovaks have and will continue to harmonize diversity. The planting of the Linden tree is a humble, yet monumental representation of their ability to reconcile divides.

To this day, Slovak ambassadors plant a Linden tree in countries across the world. Each and every Linden taking root in faraway lands is a gift of peace from the Slovak people. The Slavic symbol of love is a living message to never capitulate on hope.

SLOVAKS AND THE LIPA

are indivisible. Why? Together, they survived it all. No matter the agenda or challenge. The Linden is an expression of the mystical, mythical, religious, folkloric, cultural, political and emotional tapestry that adorns the nation.

The Linden spirit infuses the collective memory of its people. The code runs in their blood like a stream of knowledge passed on from one generation to the next. The story of every Linden tree tells the story of the face and soul of Slovakia. The Slovaks are the Lipa. The Lipa is the Slovaks.

The heart-shaped Linden leaf code captures an emotional story of Slovakia, a country that has defied all odds in breaking free from centuries of entrapment.

Today, the iron chains of the past have been shed to release the beating heart of Europe. The Slovaks have finally awoken from their slumber. With great courage, they have victoriously spread their wings.

Now you have learnt their story, follow their path and touch the destiny of a nation whose greatest achievements are yet to come.

Slovakia is rising.

EPILOGUE;
A CALL TO RETURN
TO THE HEART

Our world has been a place of perpetual competition, destruction and war. We are used to power being held in the hands of a few. Today, the era of great nations commanding our universe is coming to an end. It is becoming ever more clear that humankind is at the doorstep of unprecedented change. As the paradigms of the past are crumbling before our eyes, we must find new inspiration to create a better and more harmonious future for us all. What is to be our next blueprint?

Let us learn from our past. The Slavs in the heart of Europe have overcome much in the last two millennia. Perhaps, this time, the inspiration for global change will come from the lesser known parts of the planet, the many small nations and countries that were pushed aside as the louder voices of the dominant players rang out. These countries have a wealth of knowledge to share and it is time for the world to tune in to their delicate voices and listen.

THE STORY of the Linden and Slovakia teaches and encourages us to strive for harmony in the face of rifts, suspicion and hatred. It guides us to rise above the divides and to heal wounds through compassion, patience and understanding. Gentle Slovakia shows us that if we are to prosper on this small blue planet, we must begin to build bridges across our differences in an appreciation of all that we have in common, but also all that we can learn and teach one another.

The Slavs from the heart of Europe have a lot to offer the world. No longer invisible, they are now ready to share their knowledge. With the globe becoming ever smaller and better connected, their revelation could not be timelier. Harmonisers of divides are needed again. Born at the crossroads of worlds, Slovaks have been doing so for centuries. Today, their greatest contribution to humanity is to pass on this hereditary knowledge.

LISTEN carefully to the whisper of the Lipa tree, for it carries the wisdom of the Slovaks and the ancient Slavs. If we are to learn how to thrive and not just survive on our short journey around the sun, we must learn how to meet one another in the heart. The time has come for humanity to connect with its heart if it is ever to achieve unity and stability.

THE SLOVAK NATIONAL ANTHEM

Lightning over the Tatras

There is lightning over the Tatras
thunderclaps wildly beat.
Let us stop them, brothers,
for all that, they will disappear,
the Slovaks will revive.

That Slovakia of ours
has been fast asleep so far,
but the thunder's lightning
is rousing it
to come to.

Slovakia already arises,
tears off its shackles.
Hey/yes, dear family,
the hour has struck,
Mother Sláva/Glory is alive.

Firs are still growing
in the direction of Kriváň.
Who has feelings like a Slovak,
let him get hold of a sabre
and stand among us.

Nad Tatrou sa blýska

Nad Tatrou sa blýska
hromy divo bijú.
Zastavme ich, bratia,
veď sa ony stratia,
Slováci ožijú.

To Slovensko naše
posiaľ tvrdo spalo,
ale blesky hromu
vzbudzujú ho k tomu,
aby sa prebralo.

Už Slovensko vstáva,
putá si strháva.
Hej, rodina milá,
hodina odbila,
žije matka Sláva.

Ešte jedle rastú
na krivánskej strane.
Kto jak Slovák cíti,
nech sa šable chytí
a medzi nás stane.

THIS IS JUST THE BEGINNING...

The Legend of the Linden:
A HISTORY OF SLOVAKIA

AUTHORS' AFTERWORD; THE SECRET WORLD OF SYMBOLS AND KNOWLEDGE

HUMANKIND has always communicated using symbols. Ever since prehistoric times signs and symbols, have been used to convey and capture complex messages. Indeed, written language is a relatively recent innovation given the long history of our human race.

Long before the alphabet was invented, our ancestors created signs and symbols to pass on information and legends. From African cave paintings to European and American rock art, we can observe similar signs and symbols. Across eras and cultures, the practice of communicating through symbolism has survived.

Many thoughts, ideas and emotions are simply too expansive to capture in words alone. Imagery, on the other hand, can transcend the limitations of human language. In fact, it continues to be our civilization's most powerful communication tool.

MONEY is a perfect example of the power of symbols. Countries are very aware that the imagery found on their money can help to immortalize their achievements, heroes and victories. Family crests, national and regional emblems are created for the same purpose of anchoring memories.

Product branding is nothing more than, a use of signs and symbols to circulate messages and to incite the subconscious mind. The ancient Greek goddess of victory, Nike, was the inspiration behind the iconic athletic brand of the same name.

Depending on the context, one symbol can incite varied reactions. The fiercely independent eagle of the United States and the eagle that adorns the Nazi swastika may be comparable in image, but they convey very different messages.

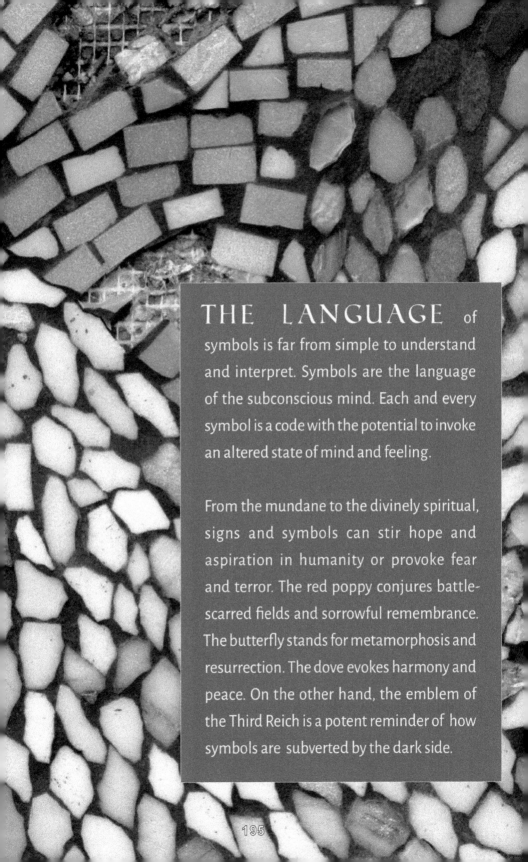

THE LANGUAGE of

symbols is far from simple to understand and interpret. Symbols are the language of the subconscious mind. Each and every symbol is a code with the potential to invoke an altered state of mind and feeling.

From the mundane to the divinely spiritual, signs and symbols can stir hope and aspiration in humanity or provoke fear and terror. The red poppy conjures battle-scarred fields and sorrowful remembrance. The butterfly stands for metamorphosis and resurrection. The dove evokes harmony and peace. On the other hand, the emblem of the Third Reich is a potent reminder of how symbols are subverted by the dark side.

Here is the **GREAT SECRET** behind symbolism. Signs and symbols represent the hidden language of the soul. The deepest, darkest and dearest of human experiences. They help humanity to express the vast unsaid and capture the even greater unseen. But if they are to be fully understood, they must be interpreted both rationally and emotionally.

Symbols speak to the heart, rather than just to the mind of humanity. The dove of peace is but an image of a bird when separated from the feelings of peace, happiness and harmony. The Olympic rings are just five overlapping circles without the sense of elation, optimism and spirit they bring.

The Linden is the mighty symbol that stores the epic of the Slovak journey. Rooted deep in the soul of the nation, it's iconic heart shaped leaf whispers the secret tale of life at the crossroads of worlds. The Linden code holds the magic of Slovakia, it is a keeper of its past, present and future.

DR ZUZANA PALOVIC

Zuzana is the daughter of Slovak emigrants. Born behind the Iron Curtain, her family fled the communist regime as political refugees to become naturalized citizens in Canada. Having spent her early childhood in the 'East', she was raised and educated in the 'West', giving Zuzana a window seat into both worlds, and by extension both consciousnesses.

Zuzana's desire to move and explore the planet expanded her horizons further. Having lived in nine countries and across four continents, Zuzana found her cosmopolitan lifestyle did nothing to erode her love for Slovakia. In fact, it only strengthened her hunger to re-discover her roots and reconnect with the country of the Linden. From science to mythology, from business to folklore, Zuzana has actively researched how the past has shaped the present of Slovakia. This mission led her into the halls of academia and into the heart of some of the best universities in the world. Dr Palovic holds a PhD from the United Kingdom.

Her work echoes the words of President Tomas Garrigue Masaryk, the visionary founding father of Czechoslovakia and her intellectual guardian. They both argue that societal change comes with a shift in individual consciousness. Zuzana is proud to be Slovak and is committed to helping empower her homeland. She is firmly determined to make sure that Slovakia's future is much greater and brighter than its fascinating past.

DR GABRIELA BEREGHAZYOVA

Gabriela's life since the earliest of childhood revolved around the magical world of storytelling. There was little entertainment available behind the Iron Curtain and so it was Slovak folk tales that first opened her mind and imagination. This shaped her destiny navigated by the family lineage, which crossed paths with the greatest Slovak storyteller of all times, Pavol Dobšinský. A childhood spent playing in the shade of Linden trees and dreaming up worlds according to Dobšinský's stories, left a mark on her mind and soul.

Gabriela's exploration into the roots of Slovak society, culture and history brought her to Slovak and British academia. This is where she had the privilege and pleasure to dedicate her doctoral research to piecing together the puzzle of Slovakia's past, present and future.

Dr Bereghazyova, an expert on corruption and Central Eastern Europe, is passionately involved in projects and initiatives that help Slovaks understand who they are. Just like Pavol Dobšinský, the father of the Slovak fairy tale, Gabriela recognizes the timeless power of stories. The ancient practice of story-telling is at the heart of her mission to help Slovaks share their knowledge with the world.

ACKNOWLEDGEMENTS

The Legend of the Linden: A History of Slovakia was fully sponsored by the generous patron Jan Telensky. Well known in the heart of Europe, his name is associated with many social initiatives, especially those committed to empowering the region and raising its international profile.

Half a century ago, fate cruelly separated young Jan from his beloved Czechoslovakia, following the Soviet invasion in the summer of 1968. He fled to England. Lost, grieving, disoriented and with no money, knowledge of English, friends or family, Jan slept in a graveyard while trying to ground himself in a new soil.

Great souls can never be deterred for long. Indeed, Jan's formidable drive and spirit saw him achieve millionaire success in England before the age of 30. But, his victory was bittersweet as he still longed for contact with his homeland. The fall of the Iron Curtain brought an opportunity. Enthusiastic to return, he was deeply disappointed by the consequences of 40 years of communism. Jan knew something had to be done about it.

Now, a quarter of a century into Slovakia's independence, Mr Telensky is very proud to be part of her progress. Thanks to the foresight and courage of his most revered venture, the award-winning luxury spa resort AquaCity in Poprad, the Slovak Tatras have received over 8 million new and curious visitors. Mr Telensky is also the president of the ice hockey club HK Poprad. Hockey is a national sport in Slovakia and its players are national treasures. Jan's support is critical to keeping this culture alive and flourishing.

Dr Telensky is a lover of Slovak mythology and folklore. He proudly boasts having a 300-year-old Linden tree in his courtyard garden. The tree reminds him of the wisdom of the ancient Slavs and the potential of the modern Slovak people.

Od rovnakých autoriek

SLOVENSKO LEGENDA LIPY

Táto kniha pozýva na sentimentálnu cestu do hĺbky slovenskej a slovanskej duše. Otvára chodníček do čarovného sveta, ktorého vstup chráni lipa. Jej posvätný srdcovitý list je šifrou nesúcou príbeh ľudí, ktorí sa zrodili na križovatke svetov.

By the same author

THE GREAT RETURN   *available on* **amazon**

In the beginning of the 21st century, Europe opened its borders to the countries from behind the Iron Curtain. Since then, over 100 million citizens, including Slovaks gained the freedom to move West without a visa. Now, a decade after the East-West exodus, our pioneers are returning home.

Telling the stories of international Slovaks who left, learned and returned, 58 voices including government, business and society share their views on the transformation of a nation. The 59th voice is that of the author, who reveals a

personal tale of loss, lessons and reconnection through a rite of passage shared by millions of people across the planet.

Time-travellers to culture-shifters, Slovakia's lost daughters and sons come home, proving that return is not just a possibility, but an opportunity.

VEĽKÝ NÁVRAT

Na začiatku 21. storočia otvorila Európa svoje hranice krajinám spoza bývalej železnej opony. Víza na západ sa stali minulosťou a viac ako 100 miliónov občanov vrátane Slovákov získalo slobodu pohybu. Po viac ako dekáde hromadných odchodov sa mnoho priekopníkov vracia zo západu domov.

Táto kniha prináša 58 hlasov z politiky, biznisu a spoločenských organizácií. Medzinárodní Slováci, ktorí odišli, spoznali a prišli späť, sa delia o svoje pohľady na prerod svojho národa. Päťdesiaty deviaty hlas patrí samotnej

autorke. Odhaľuje podmanivý osobný príbeh straty, uvedomenia a znovu nájdenia.

Dnes sa stratené dcéry a synovia Slovenska vracajú domov. Sú cestovateľmi v čase a nositeľmi zmien. Dokazujú, že návrat nie je len možnosťou, ale i nesmiernou príležitosťou.

ČESKOSLOVENSKO: ZA ŽELEZNOU OPONOU

Preneste sa na pomedzie Červenej ríše v čase ideologickej vojny, ktorá rozštiepila svet vo dvoje. Odvážte sa vstúpiť na pôdu socialistického Československa. Práve tu sa komunistický Východ a slobodný Západ ocitli nebezpečne blízko seba. Toto je príbeh obyčajných ľudí, ktorí sa zachytili do siete najväčšieho politického experimentu 20-teho storočia. To, o čom píše táto kniha si mohli len šepkať. Nahliadnite do denno-dennej reality tých, ktorých svet sa točil okolo nekompromisnej vlády kladiva a kosáka.

www.communistczechoslovakia.com

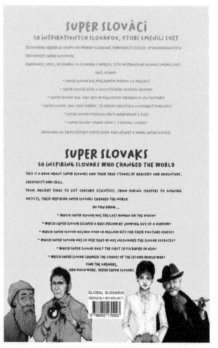

GLOBAL SLOVAKIA ACADEMY

RECLAIM YOUR ROOTS WITH OUR ONLINE COURSES

Global Slovakia provides cultural and educational programs that spotlight Slovakia's rich heritage beyond facts and figures. Using the ancient art of storytelling, we distill the known and the unknown of Slovakia into its purest essence.

Over years and decades of research and book-writing, we accumulated more stories, wisdom and material than we could fit into our books. That is why we design comprehensive, information rich, and visually stimulating online courses to share the treasures of Slovakia with you.

Global Slovakia Academy's purpose is to help you discover Slovakia, Central Europe and even greater Slavic culture, in a fun, entertaining and educational way. Our courses explore various themes from Slavic native spirituality to history, folklore, recipes and customs of Slovakia.

https://global-slovakia.teachable.com

CPSIA information can be obtained
at www.ICGtesting.com
Printed in the USA
BVHW022002040122
625469BV00019B/1396